Insight Text Guide

Diana Barnes

Into Thin Air

Jon Krakauer

First published in 2007,
reprinted 2011 by
Insight Publications Pty Ltd
ABN 57 005 102 983
89 Wellington Street,
St Kilda, Victoria 3182
Australia

Tel: +61 3 9523 0044
Fax: +61 3 9523 2044
Email: books@insightpublications.com.au

www.insightpublications.com.au

National Library of Australia Cataloguing-in-Publication entry:
Barnes, Diana, 1966- .
Jon Krakauer's Into thin air.
For secondary school students.
ISBN 9781921088735 (pbk.).
1. Krakauer, Jon. Into thin air: a personal account of
the Mount Everest disaster. I. Title.

796.522092

Printed in Australia by Ligare

contents

Character map iv

Introduction 1

Background & context 3

Genre, structure & style 8

Chapter-by-chapter analysis 11

Individuals & relationships 27

Themes, ideas & values 37

Different interpretations 48

Questions & answers 52

Sample answer 55

References & reading 57

CHARACTER MAP

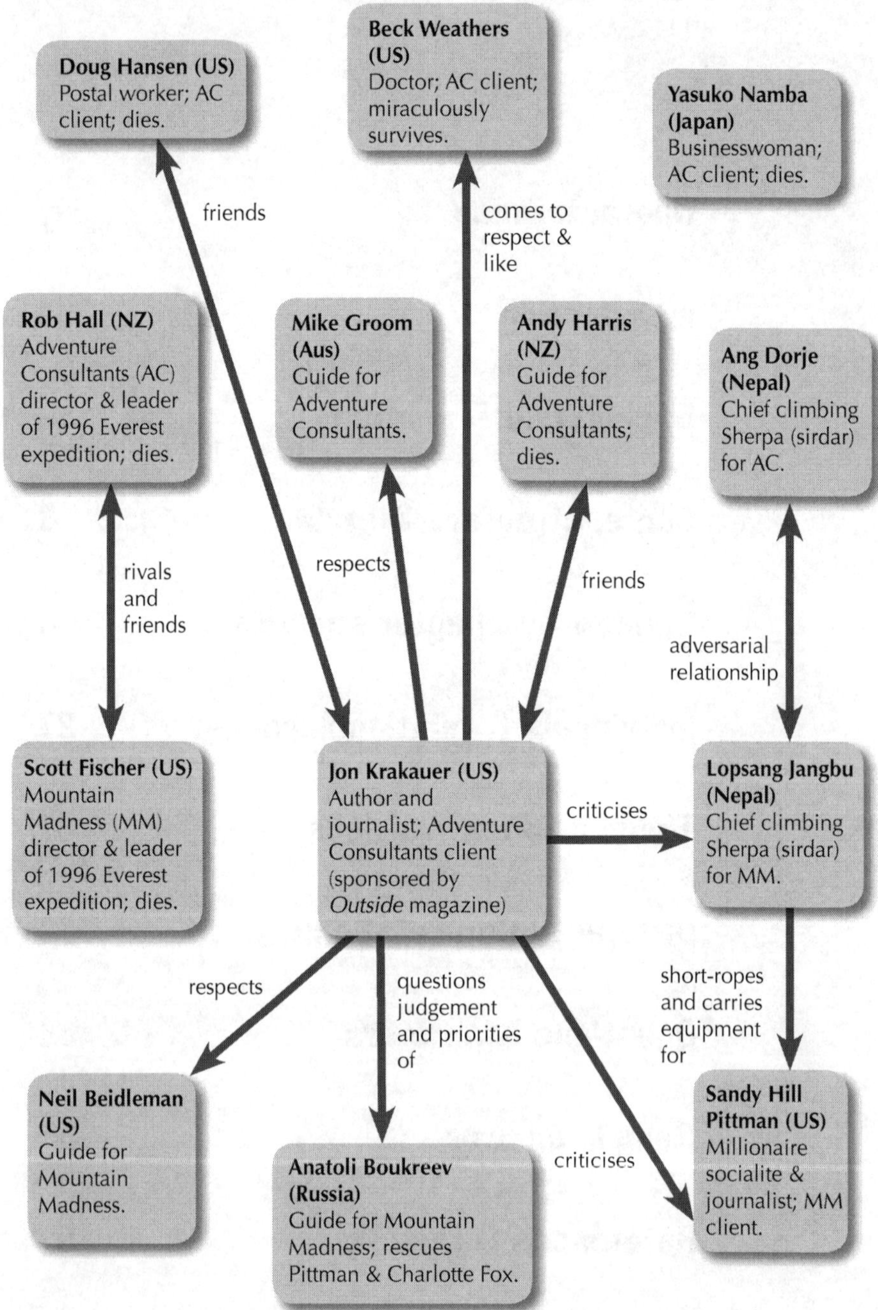

INTRODUCTION

'Climbing books, as a rule, don't live up to the drama of the climbs that produced them' writes journalist John Rothchild (2006). An instant bestseller, Jon Krakauer's *Into Thin Air: A Personal Account of the Everest Disaster* breaks this rule. This gripping reconstruction of a climbing expedition that went horribly wrong is also an illuminating analysis of the changing culture of high-altitude climbing.

Krakauer is well placed to write about mountaineering, as he was an avid climber before becoming an outdoor journalist. He has written numerous journal articles on climbing. *Into Thin Air* is his second nonfiction book. The first, *Eigar Dreams: Ventures Among Men and Mountains* (1990), is also about mountaineering; the second, *Into the Wild* (1996), is on Christopher Johnson McCandless, a man who rejected society for the Alaskan wilderness; and the most recent, *Under the Banner of Heaven: A Story of Violent Faith* (2003), is about contemporary Christian sects.

In 1996, *Outside* magazine employed Krakauer to write an article about the commercialisation of Mount Everest. *Outside* enlisted Krakauer as a client of Adventure Consultants, a commercial expedition firm: the director Rob Hall was in charge of the Everest expedition. In anticipation of the publicity and business that would be generated by Krakauer's article, Hall waived the full fee of $65 000. The expedition turned out to be disastrous for Adventure Consultants and others attempting the summit in May 1996. Nine climbers associated with the commercial expeditions died. Due to the presence of journalists Krakauer, Sandy Hill Pittman (reporting for NBC online) and Janet Bromet (reporting for *Outside Online*), the disaster made international headlines immediately.

Krakauer's *Outside* article (also entitled 'Into Thin Air') appeared a couple of months later in August 1996. It generated a heated controversy involving other eyewitnesses with different versions of events, such as Mountain Madness guide Anatoli Boukreev, who defended himself against Krakauer's savage criticism. Others who contested Krakauer's account included relatives of the deceased (for example, the family of Adventure Consultants guide Andy Harris, whose story Krakauer got wrong); and the general public, who criticised Krakauer's failure to act in the crisis and Pittman for paying for an easy passage to the summit and thereby risking others' lives.

This controversy and personal guilt motivated Krakauer to emend and expand the original article into a book-length account. *Into Thin Air* was published at the end of 1996. In 1997 Sony Pictures released a film adaptation (*Into Thin Air: Death on Everest,* dir. Robert Markowitz). In short, the drama of this 'climbing book' has certainly lived up to 'the drama ... that produced [it]'.

BACKGROUND & CONTEXT

Mountaineering

In 1923 the renowned British Climber, George Leigh Mallory, was asked why he wanted to climb Mount Everest. He quipped: "Because it is there" (p.15). Mallory's allusion to the unexplainable allure of Everest is often cited in mountaineering literature. Certainly mountains have always been there and people have always climbed them; but history reveals that the relationship between people and mountains has shifted over time. Records of people's ascents of mountains span the ages. The mummified remains of Europe's oldest Iceman, dated to 3300 BC, were found in a glacier high in the Ötztal Alps. What it meant to climb to a great height in 3300 BC and what it means in the twenty-first century are most definitely different.

The Romantic view

We see mountains as we are taught to see them. The contemporary fascination with high mountains is a product of the nineteenth-century aesthetic (of the arts) movement called **Romanticism**. Although there are exceptions, pre-Romantic writers tended to see mountains as ugly blemishes on the landscape, 'warts, and pock-holes in the face/Of th' earth' as the seventeenth-century poet John Donne (1572–1631) described them ('An Anatomy of the World: The First Anniversary', cited in Nicolson 1959, p.28). Nature was viewed as something best tamed or converted into resources. A forest represented wood for heating, stone something to be quarried for building material, and a mountain a useless obstruction and a chore to climb. Then, during the seventeenth century, following the scientific revolution, people began to understand the world and human beings' place in it differently.

This shift in attitudes paved the way for Romanticism and its avid interest in untamed nature as an elemental force, something to be appreciated for its beauty, timelessness and vastness. Mountains represented the infinite majesty of nature, what poets and philosophers called **the sublime**. As the philosopher Edmund Burke (1729–97) wrote: 'The sublime always dwells on great objects and terrible' (cited in Nicolson, p.371). Mountains were viewed as embodiments of the awe-inspiring monumental force of nature. The Romantic poet, Percy Bysshe Shelley (1792–1822) wrote:

> primeval mountains
> Teach the adverting mind. [...]
> The secret strength of things

Which governs thought, and to the infinite dome
Of heaven is as a law, inhabits thee!
('Mont Blanc', cited in Nicolson, p.388)

Gazing on mountains triggers an **epiphany**, or a moment of realisation, in which the poet recognises their place in the greater scheme. As travel became easier over the nineteenth and twentieth centuries, mountains became more accessible. Nature was regarded as tamed and no longer terrifying, but still tremendously uplifting. Romanticism has taught us to associate profound realisations – about life, nature and the cosmos – with awe-inspiring mountains.

Today's view

Today in the age of extreme adventure tourism, mountains support a number of thriving industries: commercial expeditions, films, books and outdoor equipment. Modern mountaineering involves:

- highly-developed technical skills that enable a climber to surmount rock, ice and snow
- purpose-designed equipment such as the ice-pick, crampons (spikes for climbing boots), ropes, harnesses, oxygen cylinders and heavy-duty outdoor clothing
- high-tech communication via three-way radios, the internet and satellite telephones.

Nevertheless, people continue to draw upon Romantic ideals to explain their desire to climb and to describe what they gain from the experience.

Mount Everest

The highest mountain on earth is Mount Everest, known as Jomolungma in Tibetan or Sagarmatha in Nepalese. Located in the Himalayas on the border between Tibet, Nepal and China, it is 8848 metres or 29 029 feet high. Everest is climbed either via the Southeast Ridge from Nepal or the Northeast Ridge from Tibet. The Nepalese route is a technically easier climb and therefore more frequently used, particularly by commercial expeditions. For these reasons professional mountaineers refer to it snobbishly as the 'Yak Route' (p.21). The expedition described in *Into Thin Air* took this route, but Krakauer concludes: 'Truth be told, climbing Everest has always been an extraordinarily dangerous undertaking and doubtless always will be' (p.274). Aspiring to climb Mount Everest is a relatively recent phenomenon, since Everest was not always recognised as the apex of the planet.

Key dates in Everest's history

1852 Radhanath Sikhdar, a computer (or surveyor) working on 'the Great Trigonometrical Survey of India', calculated that 'Peak XV' was 'the highest mountain in the world' (p.13).

1865 Sir Andrew Waugh, India's surveyor general, renamed Peak XV, Mount Everest after his predecessor, Sir George Everest (p.14).

1924 George Leigh Mallory and Andrew Irvine (members of a British team) got close to the summit, but bad weather closed in and they died probably without achieving their goal (pp.15–16).

1953 Edmund Hillary (New Zealand) and Tenzing Norgay (a Sherpa) on another British expedition reached the summit using bottled oxygen (p.16).

1963 Americans Tom Hornbein and Willi Unsoeld reached the summit via the difficult West Ridge (p.19).

1978 Reinhold Messner (Italy) and Peter Habeler (Austria) achieved the first summit of Everest without supplemental oxygen (p.153).

1985 Non-professional 55-year-old climber, Dick Bass, was guided to the summit of Mount Everest by David Breashears; the commerce of Everest began (p.21).

The May 1996 Everest controversy

When *Outside* commissioned Krakauer to write about commercial expeditions to Everest, it was soliciting an opinion piece on a controversy that was already raging. After Dick Bass had 'done' Everest, high-altitude climbing culture changed irrevocably. Traditional high-altitude climbing expeditions were national state-funded affairs involving experienced professional mountaineers, such as Mallory or Hillary. By contrast, in the commercial era – of Adventure Consultants, Mountain Madness or Alpine Ascents – clients pay to join an expedition organised and guided by professional mountaineers.

Some traditionalists (including Hillary) criticise commercial ventures for taking inexperienced people into such dangerous situations (p.34). Other professionals recognise the risks involved, but they see commercial guiding as a livelihood, as state-funding for expeditions dwindles (Boukreev 1997). Krakauer expresses grave ethical concerns about the risks involved. He proposes that different rules must be applied to professional and commercial ventures, and that what is appropriate for experienced professionals is too risky for novices. In an age of extreme adventure tourism, *Into Thin Air* addresses these pressing concerns directly.

Anatoli Boukreev's response

Krakauer's conclusions about the conflict between traditional and commercial climbing practices lead him to criticise Anatoli Boukreev, Mountain Madness's guide. According to Krakauer, Boukreev:

- was the product of an old-style tough Soviet climbing culture and did not grasp the expectations of Western clients
- frequently left his clients to fend for themselves
- undermined his capacity to care for his clients at high altitudes by forgoing supplemental oxygen
- focused upon his own climb rather than guiding.

Boukreev justified his behaviour in May 1996 in a letter to *Outside* magazine. When *Outside* refused to publish it due to its length, Boukreev (assisted by G. Weston DeWalt) wrote his own best-selling book about the disaster: *The Climb: Tragic Ambitions on Everest* (1997). In it Boukreev describes Soviet climbing culture and how it ill-prepared him for Western expectations. He argues that Krakauer and others misinterpreted his lack of fluency in English as stand-offishness. He explains how his strict acclimatisation regime prepared him to climb without oxygen, but that he carried oxygen to use if needed. He argues that by not using oxygen, he could perform better as a guide because he did not have to adjust suddenly when oxygen supplies ran out (as happened in May 1996).

Boukreev explains that he left the Mountain Madness clients: when they were climbing well; under direct orders of expedition leader, Scott Fischer; to perform work behind the scenes (such as securing ropes, or setting up camp, necessary because the expedition was short-staffed) of which Krakauer was ignorant; and to conserve his energy in case of a disaster. He also describes his frustration that Fischer did not respect his experience and authority when he proposed a more rigorous acclimatisation regime, and when he judged that the weather was too unstable to attempt the summit on May 10, 1996.

David Breashears's response

Breashears and the IMAX team were on Mount Everest in May 1996 to shoot an IMAX (wide format) film and he was involved in the rescue of Adventure Consultants client, Beck Weathers and Taiwanese expedition leader, Makalu Gau. Breashears is a film director, an elite professional climber, and the first guide to take an amateur (Bass) to the summit. His book, *High Exposure: An Enduring Passion for Everest and Unforgiving Places* (1999), is an autobiographical account of his mountaineering and filmmaking career.

Breashears gives a fascinating account of professional mountaineering culture. He mentions the May 1996 disaster both in his introduction and the final chapters. Breashears was a witness and not a victim of the disaster and this gives him a different perspective. His account differs from Krakauer's in a number of respects. He outlines the code of conduct required for guiding non-professionals and points to where Hall, Fischer and Boukreev failed it. Breashears stresses his respect for Hall's skills and meticulousness, but he feels that Hall saw himself as invincible and downplayed the risks facing amateur climbers. The IMAX team was scheduled to reach the summit of Everest the day before Adventure Consultants and Mountain Madness, but Breashears had ordered the team to descend due to unstable weather. Breashears also provides more sympathetic portraits of wealthy amateur climbers vilified in the media, in particular Pittman and Bass.

Beck Weathers's version

In 2000 Weathers's story, *Left for Dead: My Journey Home from Everest* (written with Stephen G. Michaud) was published. This book focuses less on the professional versus amateur controversy and more on Weathers's remarkable near-death experience, rescue, and his long struggle after amputations and a nose reconstruction. His experience triggered a profound and life-changing realisation. He affirms the accounts given by Krakauer and Breashears, and reiterates their criticisms of Fischer's carelessness and Boukreev's failure to use oxygen. As a practising pathologist, Weathers gives a medical perspective on the effects of altitude on the body. He also adds a few humorous anecdotes of his own.

And ...

The most recent eyewitness account appears in Ed Viesturs's autobiography, *No Shortcut to the Top: Climbing the World's 14 Highest Peaks* (2006, written with David Roberts). Viesturs was involved in the IMAX project (directed by Breashears) and the rescue of Beck Weathers and Makalu Gau.

GENRE, STRUCTURE & STYLE

Genre

Into Thin Air is primarily classified as a work of nonfiction, or fact, but it draws upon many different genres both fictional and nonfictional. The primary organisational principle is the timeline, or historical sequence of events: this is signalled in the chapter headings. In addition, each chapter begins with a quotation from another text; some of these texts are classics of outdoor literature about climbing Everest, while others are works of literature, philosophy and psychology. These multiple and varied quotations give *Into Thin Air* textual affiliations, or a heritage, which explain its ideas and writing style.

Nonfiction

Into Thin Air is classified as **nonfiction**, a genre of writing that expresses facts that the author believes to be true. By contrast, fiction is invented by the author and does not claim to be true. Both fiction and nonfiction, however, must have a narrative, or a story-line. Nonfiction strives to persuade the reader of the truth of its story; in other words, it presents an argument to convince readers. It must demonstrate its trustworthiness by documenting its sources of information, such as by acknowledging references, giving eyewitness accounts, and naming authorities (and explaining why they are trustworthy).

As a work of nonfiction, *Into Thin Air*:

- investigates a real event, or series of events
- presents an argument supporting its interpretation of events
- strives to convince its reader of the veracity (truth) of its interpretation
- includes a bibliography
- names eyewitnesses cited
- demonstrates the trustworthiness of other authorities it uses.

Outdoor literature

Outdoor literature is a **sub-genre** (or sub-category) of nonfiction that has become increasingly prominent over the past century. There are many different forms of outdoor writing and *Into Thin Air* draws from a rich variety of generic possibilities. For instance:

- like **travel writing**, it describes exotic places and customs
- like **adventure or quest literature**, its protagonists (central characters) seek an almost unattainable personal and public goal

- like **exploration literature**, it recounts a dangerous expedition into unknown and dangerous terrain
- like **romantic literature**, it describes the awe and fear inspired by nature.

Mountaineering books constitute a growing category within outdoor literature; many focus upon Mount Everest.

Personal account

Krakauer's original journal article was entitled 'Into Thin Air', whereas the book is called *Into Thin Air: A Personal Account of the Everest Disaster*. The second part of the book title identifies it as a personal account. A personal work of nonfiction may seem like a contradiction in terms, but it signals that Krakauer is putting forward the truth as best he can, based on his own personal experience. He is not claiming that this is a definitive account. This is a qualification (or modification) of his original title. The new title makes it clear that this is one person's interpretation of the truth.

Krakauer's prior personal experience is woven into the narrative of *Into Thin Air*. For example, when Krakauer gives a history of climbing Mount Everest he runs through certain key dates and events, then turns to his own boyhood Everest dreams. He mentions books, people and experiences that stimulated his own aspirations and shaped his attitudes. These details are **autobiographical**, or drawn from his life. By including them, Krakauer signals his own biases (or prejudices). *Into Thin Air* is a **subjective** narrative; in other words, it is told from one person's perspective. Krakauer tries to indicate his biases honestly, so that readers can judge his interpretation of events for themselves.

Structure

Into Thin Air has a roughly chronological structure. Chapter titles each note a time and place to help readers navigate the multiple versions of events. Chapter 1 describes Krakauer's arrival upon the summit of Mount Everest, then after Chapter 2 (on historical background) the chapters describe the events leading up to the expedition, the drama of the expedition and its aftermath. It returns to the summit day a number of times:

- Chapters 14 and 15 give further depth
- Chapter 17 reconstructs the stories of fellow climbers
- Chapter 18 describes expeditions on the other side of the mountain.

Into Thin Air attempts to pin down exactly what happened but, as Krakauer explains, this task is complicated by the fact that high-altitude memories are notoriously unreliable. The chronological doubling-back in the narrative is a means of piecing together a number of different accounts in order to get closer to the truth.

Framing the narrative

Introductory and concluding materials frame the narrative of *Into Thin Air*. Krakauer respectfully dedicates the book to his wife and the memory of his deceased co-climbers. The list of 'Dramatis Personæ' acknowledges a myriad of other experiences of and perspectives on Everest in May 1996. Similarly, in the concluding 'Author's Note' Krakauer acknowledges many people who aided his writing. The 'Selected Bibliography' lists some of the references cited. Together these framing materials present Krakauer's position (as one opinion amongst many) and support his authority (by demonstrating the authorities – people and books – upon which he draws).

Chapter structures

The chapter titles mark chronological advances in the narrative, and geographic steps up or down the mountain. These steps are also conceptual progressions towards understanding the disaster. To this end the chapters draw upon a range of background materials, and open with a quotation drawn from another text that puts events into a wider context. The chapters do not simply retell the story of the disaster; they provide a means of interpreting a dimension of the story. This is done in a number of ways, including Krakauer's retrospective judgements; background information on climbing culture; and discussion of other relevant topics and quotations.

Use of quotations

Each chapter begins with a quotation covering a related topic. Most of the quotations derive from other writing about Mount Everest (by Thomas F. Hornbein, Walt Unsworth, Eric Shipton or George Leigh Mallory) or climbing. Some come from accounts of other dangerous expeditions (such as Apsley Cherry-Garrard or Robert Falcon Scott on Antarctica). Poetry and a novel are cited (for example, by W. B. Yeats and Joseph Conrad). Krakauer also quotes from A. Alvarez's book about the link between the death drive and art. These quotations draw the reader's attention to a key theme in each chapter (see the chapter-by-chapter analyses below).

CHAPTER-BY-CHAPTER ANALYSIS

Preface (pp.XI–XXII)

Summary: *Krakauer's personal involvement.*

Krakauer explains the difficulties of writing *Into Thin Air* in personal terms. In particular, he draws our attention to his:

- desire to get the story right and correct errors in the *Outside* article
- sense of being crippled by emotion and guilt over his own role
- feeling that he is trying to 'purge Everest from [his] life' (p.XII)
- lack of distance – he was advised to wait until he had some perspective on the events but he did not.

Key point

Krakauer presents his lack of objectivity as a strength: 'I wanted my account to have a raw, ruthless sort of honesty that seemed in danger of leaching away with the passage of time and the dissipation of anguish' (p.XIII).

Q How does Krakauer characterise himself as a writer?

Q What are the advantages and disadvantages of a raw and honest narrative style?

Chapter 1: Everest Summit; May 10, 1996 (pp.3–9)

Summary: *Krakauer on the summit of Mount Everest numb, cold and tired; why did disaster strike?*

Key theme: modern climbers are complacent about risk.

Eric Shipton observes that in 'our age of easy mechanical conquest. ... [w]e had forgotten that the mountain still holds the master card' (*Upon That Mountain*, 1938, cited p.5). By opening with this quotation, Krakauer suggests that the expedition with which he was involved also suffered from complacency; that he and others downplayed the dangers of such an arduous climb, even though the very real risks give high-altitude mountaineering 'its deep fascination', as Shipton suggests. Accordingly, in the opening paragraph when Krakauer describes his own arrival at the summit of Everest, he emphasises his sense of ennui, or boredom. Although the view is spectacular, he is too exhausted to care.

Krakauer asks: 'why, if the weather had begun to deteriorate, had climbers on the upper mountain not heeded the signs?' (p.6). He suggests the following answers:

- the clouds visible from the summit resembled typical 'harmless puffs of convection' (p.7), but unpredictable swells of treacherous weather are typical at high altitudes
- the congestion of climbers prevented rapid descent
- oxygen-starved climbers do not make rational decisions
- climbers were too exhausted or hypoxic (oxygen starved) to think, too busy 'memorializ[ing] their arrival at the apex of the planet' (p.9), or too inexperienced to identify changing conditions.

Q What are the signs of impending disaster?

Q On the summit climbers play roles they have rehearsed in their minds. To what extent do their expectations blind them to reality?

Chapter 2: Dehra Dun, India; 1852 (pp.11–26)

Summary: *The history of Mount Everest; Krakauer's boyhood dream develops into an obsession; commercialisation of Everest; Krakauer remains eager to ascend Everest.*

Key theme: the persistence of boyhood dreams and masculine ideals.

In the prefatory quotation, Thomas F. Hornbein recalls how a picture book stimulated his desire to climb Mount Everest. He speculates that the dream of climbing Everest 'was there for many boys and grown men to aspire toward' (*Everest: The West Ridge*, 1966, cited p.13).

Key point

Books generate the dreams and ideals – adventure, bravery and victory against all odds – that motivate men to climb Everest in the face of certain danger.

Masculine ideals are emphasised in the history of Everest as Krakauer summarises it. The following points identify a number of these ideals.

- **Naming and Empire:** when Everest was renamed to honour an English man, the surveyor general, Sir George Everest, the masculine bureaucratic culture of the English Empire was stamped onto the landscape displacing indigenous names and meanings, e.g. the Tibetan 'Jomolungma' ('goddess, mother of the world') and the Nepalese 'Sagarmatha' ('goddess of the sky') (p.14).

- **Ideals change:** the portrait of 1920s climber, George Leigh Mallory and his companions reading Shakespeare invokes a bygone notion of manly recreation (p.16).
- **Empire reborn:** the 1953 Hillary/Norgay ascent coincided with the coronation of Elizabeth II. The two events were celebrated together as evidence that Britain was 'Emerging at last from the austerity' that followed World War II, the decolonisation of the British Empire and Britain's loss of world power (Morris, cited p.18).
- **Boyhood dreams:** shared by Krakauer (p.20).
- **Climbing ethos:** of 'intense competition and undiluted machismo' (p.20).
- **Buy the dream:** Dick Bass's 1985 ascent 'spurred a swarm of other weekend climbers to follow in his guided bootprints, and rudely pulled Everest into the postmodern era' (pp.21–2).

Q How important are boyhood dreams and masculine ideals to Krakauer's history of Everest?

Q What role do you think masculine ideals played in the tragedy of May 1996?

Chapter 3: Over Northern India; March 29, 1996 (pp.27–38)

Summary: *Krakauer arrives at Kathmandu; meets guide Andy Harris and leader Rob Hall; Hall's climbing history; expedition group meets; Krakauer's concerns about a group climb.*

Key themes: the commercial group expedition.

This chapter opens with an interesting parable about climbing written by twentieth-century British climber, John Menlove Edwards. Edwards's description of a climbing obsession in Neptune – 'people [...] spent their spare time and all their energies in chasing the clouds of their own glory up and down all the steepest faces in the district' ('Letter from a Man', cited p.29) – could describe the Adventure Consultants group. Krakauer conveys his uneasiness about the group's lack of mountaineering experience.

Q What are Krakauer's concerns about group climbing?

Q How accurately do Krakauer's early concerns anticipate the disaster?

Chapter 4: Phakding; March 31, 1996 (pp.39–54)

Summary: *Trek through Sherpa villages; Western attitudes towards Sherpas; Tenzing Sherpa injured.*

Key theme: Western misunderstandings of Sherpa culture.

Krakauer cites Hornbein's description of the circularity of the Everest quest: 'I wondered if I had not come a long way only to find that what I really sought was something I had left behind' (*Everest: The West Ridge,* cited p.41). This suggests that Westerners climb Everest in search of answers to their lives at home.

Key point

The Romantic quest for an epiphany blinds climbers to the realities and values of Sherpa culture.

Q How does Krakauer urge his readers to question the dream of Everest?

Q How does questioning the Everest dream prepare us for Krakauer's interpretation of the disaster of May 1996?

Chapter 5: Lobuje; April 8, 1996 (pp.55–70)

Summary: *Rescue of Tenzing; Harris unwell; arrival at Everest Base Camp; Scott Fischer and Mountain Madness; realities of high-altitude life.*

Key theme: the landscape's indifference to humans.

Although Hornbein describes a world 'not intended for human habitation' (*Everest: The West Ridge,* cited p.57), Everest Base Camp is a community that 'bustled like an anthill' (p.60). It comprises at least 300 tents and headquarters for the commercial ventures. The Adventure Consultants camp is not just a repository for supplies and medical assistance; it also offers remarkable creature comforts. Regardless, life at high altitude is not comfortable. The symptoms of mild altitude sickness – insomnia, loss of appetite, gastric distress and severe headaches – strike most climbers while their bodies acclimatise (p.69).

Hall gives advice generously, even to his competitors. He is confident in his staged acclimatisation plan and jokingly shrugs off Krakauer's doubts.

Key point

Base Camp culture entrenches Hall's authority and status. Clients are encouraged to relinquish their own faculties of judgement and defer to the leader's greater expertise and authority.

Q According to Krakauer, Hall is likable, yet Hall uses humour to undermine those who question his authority. Do you find this behaviour likable?

Q How are women positioned by the masculine culture of mountaineering at the Everest Base Camp and on the slopes?

Chapter 6: Everest Base Camp; April 12, 1996 (pp.71–84)

Summary: *Hall's plan; preparing for day-trip to Camp One; commodification of Everest; Krakauer's altitude sickness.*

Key theme: risk.

Krakauer invokes the authority of American psychologist A. Alvarez to suggest that danger is integral to climbing and 'serves merely to sharpen [the climber's] awareness and control' (*The Savage God*, 1972, cited p.73).

Preparing for the first climb, Krakauer feels concerned that his team-mates are ill-prepared (new boots and lack of training, pp.74–5). Although the Western Cwm (pronounced coom) is a gentle climb, on Khumbu Glacier tottering *seracs*, or huge blocks of ice, are challenging. This exposes the group's lack of skills.

Krakauer suggests that climbing Everest was quite different from his previous climbing experience: 'more like a mammoth construction project than climbing as I'd previously known it' (p.73). He also identifies the following two differences:

- usually a climber relies upon intuition, but Krakauer is so terrified that he cannot judge cool-headedly
- usually mountaineers attach themselves to one another for safety, but on Everest climbers clip themselves directly to the rock face.

Q 'Hall … was a quartermaster nonpareil' (p.73). What evidence do you see of good leadership in this chapter?

Q When Krakauer mentions his wife's concerns, he puts the risks undertaken by the climbers in a broader context. How is this theme developed across the book?

Chapter 7: Camp One; April 13, 1996 (pp.85–100)

Summary: *A history of misguided Everest climbers; credentials of clients.*

Key theme: the delusional pull of Everest.

The two quotations opening this chapter signal the eccentric and even deluded states of mind that can characterise those who attempt to climb Everest. For Walt Unsworth, Everest attracts 'men for whom the unattainable has a special attraction' (*Everest,* 1991, cited p.87); for Earl Denman, the source of the attraction lies in discovering 'what could be accomplished by means of tenacity and little else' (*Alone to Everest,* 1954, cited p.87).

Krakauer describes the idealism and delusional states of two early-twentieth-century climbers, Denman and Maurice Wilson:

- Earl Denman, a Canadian engineer, attempted Everest in 1947 accompanied by Tenzing Norgay. Norgay wrote: 'Any man in his right mind would have said no. But I couldn't say no. For in my heart I needed to go' (cited p.88).
- A member of Eric Shipton's 1935 expedition wrote of the discovery of the body of Maurice Wilson: 'he was, after all, doing much the same as ourselves, his tragedy seemed to have been brought a little too near home for us' (Charles Warren, cited p.90).

Successful climbers are also under the spell of Everest: Krakauer jokes that 'half the population at Base Camp was clinically delusional' (p.88).

Key point

The dream of climbing Mount Everest stimulates men to run headfirst into danger; the era of extreme tourism has made the dream more widely available. The 'marginally qualified dreamers' (p.90) flooding the mountain are ill-prepared to assess the real dangers. Krakauer asks who should be on the mountain: the experienced, the wealthy or the professionals?

Q Who does Krakauer think should climb Everest?

Q Krakauer includes Hall's comment that: "With so many incompetent people on the mountain … I think it's pretty unlikely that we'll get through this season without something bad happening up high" (p.100). Does Hall recognise his own drive towards danger?

Chapter 8: Camp One; April 16, 1996 (pp.101–19)

Summary: *Second acclimatisation exercise; trek to Camps One and Two; encounter dead bodies; return to Base Camp; the South African team; Ngawang Topche collapses.*

Key theme: high-altitude hardship is more acute for some.
Stressing the physical and mental hardship of climbing Everest, Eric Shipton writes: 'I doubt if anyone would claim to enjoy life at high altitudes', where mind and body become 'dull and unresponsive' (*Upon That Mountain,* cited p.103). In this chapter Krakauer describes his own experience of the physical discomfort of the brutal cold and scorching heat, and the mental shock at seeing frozen bodies along the route (p.106).

This chapter provides a critical social perspective on the physical and emotional hardships of ascending the world's highest mountain as follows:

- Krakauer is emasculated and pathetically weakened (p.104).
- Sherpa hardship: Ngawang Topche suffers severe altitude sickness but is reluctant to withdraw for fear of reducing future work opportunities.
- Social climber: New York socialite Sandy Hill Pittman's luggage – computers, solar panels and an espresso machine – transported by Sherpas.

Q Describe Krakauer's racial and social analysis of the hardships of altitude.

Q How relevant are the issues of class and privilege when disaster strikes?

Chapter 9: Camp Two; April 28, 1996 (pp.121–31)

Summary: *Climb from Camp Two to Camp Three; abandon climb due to bad weather; Doug Hansen depressed over ill health; depressing news of Ngawang Topche's deterioriating health; Buddhist superstition.*

Key theme: the role and craft of storytelling.

Key point

Joan Didion's words in the prefatory quotation encourage readers to view this book as a construction based on real events, rather than the absolute and complete truth. Like

Didion, Krakauer imposes 'ideas' or 'a narrative line upon [the] disparate images ... [of] actual experience' (The White Album, 1979, cited p.123).

Krakauer observes that: 'It seemed increasingly unsafe to keep going up' (p.125). Hall level-headedly turns the team back.

Q Does Krakauer give more weight to the human failings that contributed to the disaster than to the Sherpas' beliefs?

Q In this chapter Hall makes a good decision, but how are later bad decisions anticipated in Krakauer's narrative?

Chapter 10: Lhotse Face; April 29, 1996 (pp.133–42)

Summary: *Krakauer's growing respect for team-mates; his qualms as a journalist; visit Camp Three; a case of HACE; return to Base Camp before final summit push.*

Key theme: journalistic reporting as a mode of storytelling.
Through the daily 'toil, tedium, and suffering' (p.136), Krakauer gains respect for his co-climbers and questions his role as a journalist.

HACE (High Altitude Cerebral Edema, or Oedema) strikes Dale Kruse, a Mountain Madness client. Kruse recalls: "my mind wasn't working, although it wasn't apparent to me ... It was like I was very drunk ... I couldn't walk without stumbling, and completely lost the ability to think or speak" (p.140). Importantly for Krakauer's account of later events, the survivor emphasises how the condition compromises his judgement and develops rapidly.

Journalists' Code of Ethics

It is interesting to consider Krakauer's reservations about his role as a journalist on this expedition in the light of a code of ethics for journalists. The (US) Society of Professional Journalists Code of Ethics includes the following two principles:

- Seek Truth and Report It – Journalists should be honest, fair and courageous in gathering, reporting and interpreting information.
- Minimise Harm – Ethical journalists treat sources, subjects and colleagues as human beings deserving of respect ... (http://www.spj.org/ethicscode.asp).

Q Does *Into Thin Air* adhere to the principles of the Journalists' Code of Ethics?

Q 'Climbing was like life itself, only it was cast in much sharper relief' (p.137). What does Krakauer mean by this?

Chapter 11: Base Camp; May 6, 1996 (pp.143–56)

Summary: *Begin summit push; Fischer ailing; Boukreev's guiding style; the supplemental oxygen debate; Chen Yu-Nan dies.*

Key theme: mountain ethics.

David Roberts asks: 'How much of the appeal of mountaineering lies in its simplification of interpersonal relationships … its substitution of an Other (the mountain, the challenge) for the relationship itself?' (cited p.145). This question focuses the chapter's investigation of mountain ethics in relation to the following issues.

- Anatoli Boukreev 'did not believe in coddling the weak' (p.149) and, in Krakauer's view, failed as a guide.
- The supplemental oxygen debate: some 'purists' (p.153) see using bottled oxygen as a failure to meet the challenge of altitude. Krakauer argues guides should use it to ensure that they are mentally and physically capable of fulfilling their duty of care. Unlike Boukreev, Groom and Hall used it on principle (p.154).
- A death on the mountain: when Makalu Gau, the Taiwanese expedition leader, learned that his friend Chen Yu-Nan died, he immediately 'assured his team that Chen's death would in no way affect their plans to leave for the summit at midnight' (p.156).
- Ethical dilemma anticipated: commending Göran Kropp, a Swedish soloist who turned back just an hour before the summit judging that he needed his energy for the descent, Hall remarked: "any bloody idiot can get *up* this hill … The trick is to get back down alive" (p.147). At the same time, Doug Hansen 'was hell-bent on joining the summit push' (p.148).

Key point

These two elements are connected, as Hall later misjudges the consequences of helping Hansen fulfil his Everest dream. In doing so he fails his duty of care in a way he could not anticipate.

Q Should ethical standards change at altitude?

Q How does Hansen's mental and physical state later create an ethical dilemma for Hall?

Chapter 12: Camp Three; May 9, 1996 (pp.157–70)

Summary: *Leave Camp Three; adjusting to supplemental oxygen; arrive at Camp Four; bad storm; Fischbeck turns back; Hansen turns back but then continues; Hall's group protocols frustrate Krakauer; Lopsang Jangbu short-ropes Pittman.*

Key theme: the momentum upward is strong and small warnings are ignored. Hornbein's observation that 'Too much labor, too many sleepless nights, and too many dreams had been invested' (*Everest: The West Ridge*, cited p.159) helps to explain the irrational push to the summit despite several serious problems. Climbing congestion (p.159), hypothermia (p.160), sleep deprivation and ill omens (Fischbeck's intuition, p.165) all threaten the expedition's success.

Unwell, Hansen struggles on summit day but continues after talking with Hall (p.165). Hall's policy of travelling as a group causes some clients to wait around getting cold and wasting precious time and oxygen (pp.166–7).

The climbers cannot see the mounting problems because they are exhausted, oxygen-deprived and focused upon the climb; moreover, the clients are encouraged to be passive rather than to challenge the judgement of their guides (p.168).

Q Was there really 'too much invested to quit' in the situation Krakauer describes?

Q This chapter is almost entirely focused on the unfolding events. How does this shift in narrative style affect the mood and pace?

Chapter 13: Southeast Ridge; May 10, 1996 (pp.171–81)

Summary: *Leave Camp Four for the summit; rope lines not installed as planned; traffic jam; time is running out; Hutchison, Taske and Kasischke turn back; benefits of oxygen; time wasted before lines installed; the summit.*

Key theme: 'all the talk of an easy snow slope is a myth' (George Mallory, letter to his wife, cited p.173).

That disaster was imminent is evident in retrospect. Ang Dorje sees ghosts and fears something is wrong (p.175). Things do not go to plan: there is 'bottleneck' traffic (p.175) and ropes are not in place to assist clients. After waiting, Beidleman, Harris and Krakauer fix the ropes themselves but each climber only has eighteen hours of oxygen (p.179).

Personal flaws also contribute to the climbers' problems: Namba is so driven that she 'nearly caused a disaster' (p.176); Boukreev and Lopsang forgo supplemental oxygen (p.178); and Hall fails to specify the turn-around time (p.177). When the summit is still three hours away, Hutchison, Taske and Kasischke turn back (p.177), yet others continue.

Q 'I found myself atop a slender wedge of ice ... with nowhere higher to climb' (p.180). Why is the summit such an anticlimax?

Q 'Above the South Col, up in the Death Zone, survival is to no small degree a race against the clock' (p.173). Explain what Krakauer means by this.

Chapter 14: Summit; 1.12 PM, May 10, 1996 (pp.183–95)

Summary: *Krakauer, Harris and Boukreev at the summit; clouds in sight; Krakauer waits to descend and runs out of oxygen; the difficult descent; Harris in trouble; Krakauer arrives at Camp Four exhausted.*

Key theme: altitude dulls the will to climb.
Reinhold Messner's description (in the prefatory quotation from *The Crystal Horizon*, 1989) of the indifference resulting from oxygen deprivation partially explains people's failure to respond appropriately to the situation.

From the summit Krakauer notices 'wispy clouds' (p.185) that later develop into a blizzard. Anxious about his oxygen supply, he is focused entirely on descending safely. He is frustrated by traffic that slows his descent, and he feels drugged when his oxygen runs out (p.186).

Key point

Krakauer emphasises his impaired mental condition: 'Dizzy, fearing that I would black out' (p.187); 'my punch-drunk state' (p.191); 'I observed my own slide from reality with a blend of fascination and horror' (p.193). These comments explain his failure to register Harris's worsening condition.

Q Indifference experienced at the time contrasts with passion felt in retrospect. How does the tension between the remembered experience and the retrospective interpretation shape how the story is told?

Q 'Given what unfolded ... the ease with which I abdicated responsibility ... was a lapse that's likely to haunt me for the rest of my life' (p.188). Discuss.

Chapter 15: Summit; 1.25 PM, May 10, 1996 (pp.197–214)

Summary: *Clients and guides arrive on the summit then begin the difficult descent; 6.45 pm storm hits; Beidleman's group disorientated; Boukreev and Hutchison attempt rescue; Namba seems dead; Boukreev rescues Fox and Pittman; Madsen follows; Weathers assumed dead.*

Key theme: the human dimension to the tragedy.

This chapter reconstructs events in the storm which Krakauer did not experience. Although Krakauer invokes the 'sinister violence of intention' of some gales (Joseph Conrad, *Lord Jim*, 1900, cited p.199), he focuses on the human contributions to the disastrous outcome. These include his own failure to act, Fischer's exhaustion, the lack of radios, rescue coordination problems and Boukreev's decision to return to camp ahead of his clients.

Q What makes heroes of Boukreev, Beidleman and Madsen?

Q How do the guiding styles of Beidleman and Boukreev differ?

Chapter 16: South Col; 6.00 AM, May 11, 1996 (pp.215–20)

Summary: *At 6 am Harris is missing; Krakauer identifies Harris's footprints; Adams remembers differently.*

Key theme: the slipperiness of memory.

American journalist Harold Brodkey writes: 'I distrust summaries ... any too great a claim that one is in control of what one recounts' ('Manipulations', cited p.217). This quotation anticipates the structure of the chapter and the raw style in which it is written.

Krakauer recollects seeing Harris near Camp Four and then searching for him. He realises that Harris may have stumbled over a cliff to his death. Adams's memory of events, however, suggests that Krakauer mistook Adams for Harris. Krakauer is stunned; he asks: 'Was I really so debilitated that I had stared into the face of a near stranger and mistaken him for a friend ...?' (p.220).

Krakauer's mistaken memory is complicated by the fact that he made his story public and hurt Harris's partner, family and friends.

Q Krakauer regrets the pain his error caused. Does he see this as an ethical issue? Do you?

Q Knowing his memory is impaired, how does Krakauer try to ensure the truthfulness of his version of events?

Chapter 17: Summit; 3.40 PM, May 10, 1996 (pp.221–35)

Summary: *At 3.40 pm Fischer, Lopsang Jangbu, Gau and two Sherpas leave the summit; 4 pm Hall and Hansen leave the summit but are soon in trouble; Harris helps; Fischer in trouble; Gau rescued; Hansen and Harris die; Hall talks with his wife; he dies.*

Key theme: the dead cannot tell their story.

Just before his death, Robert Scott wrote: 'Had we lived, I should have had a tale to tell of the hardihood, endurance, and courage of my companions ... These rough notes and our dead bodies must tell the tale' ('Message to the Public', Antarctica 1912, cited p.223). This draws attention to the difficulty of reconstructing the experience of the dead. Krakauer emphasises the following gaps:

- Although Hall is fastidious, he contravenes his own plan of leaving the summit no later than 2 pm (and leaves at 4 pm)
- When Hall radios Base Camp, he cannot account for what happened to Harris and Hansen
- Discussions with Hall during his final hours do not illuminate why he makes no attempt to descend
- Fischer, Hansen and Harris die without making radio contact.

Key point

Krakauer can only speculate on what motivated Hall's decisions in the crisis: hypoxia, or perhaps a misguided sense of duty to Hansen.

Q How does this chapter underline the human cost of the Everest dream?

Q Hall's final conversation with his wife, Jan Arnold, makes the tragedy seem more real – but should such private moments be made public?

Chapter 18: Northeast Ridge; May 10, 1996 (pp.237–42)

Summary: *Indo-Tibetan Border Police expedition struggles in the storm; a Japanese party leaves them to die.*

Key theme: mountain ethics.

Krakauer's narrative shifts geographically to the Tibetan side of Everest to describe concurrent expeditions of the Indo-Tibetan Border Police and a Japanese group. This side of the mountain offers the Northeast Ridge,

Mallory's route. Three members of the Indo-Tibetan Border Police expedition struggle in the storm. A Japanese group pass the struggling climbers without offering assistance other than to free a climber who had become entangled in a rope. Afterwards the Japanese leader Shigekawa explained: "We were too tired to help. Above 8,000 meters is not a place where people can afford morality" (p.241).

Key point

Discussing the problems confronted by two other groups puts ethics into sharper focus, suggesting that perhaps Krakauer finds it easier to judge strangers.

Q How adequate is Shigekawa's explanation?

Q How does the shift towards the other side of the mountain fit into the narrative of *Into Thin Air*?

Chapter 19: South Col; 7.30 AM, May 11, 1996 (pp.243–56)

Summary: *Camp Four: Krakauer's distress; Hutchison takes charge; Namba and Weathers found just alive; a Sherpa killed; IMAX and Alpine Ascents help; Weathers returns to Camp; Beidleman and clients descend to Camp Three; Krakauer and others prepare to descend.*

Key theme: incomprehension and shock.
The prefatory quotation is from W. B. Yeats's poem 'The Second Coming' (1920), which describes a dizzying spiral movement: 'Things fall apart; the centre cannot hold ... The ceremony of innocence is drowned' (cited p.245). Yeats expresses the apocalyptic mood following World War I, when everything known and trusted seemed to collapse. This is the spirit of Krakauer's dawning realisation 'of what had happened – of what was still happening' and he experiences 'the downward spiral into the nightmarish territory of the mad' (p.245).

Hutchison organises a search and makes critical decisions. When Namba and Weathers are found almost dead, he leaves them in the ice and snow. Other survivors (including Krakauer) support his decision. Then Weathers stumbles into the camp terribly frostbitten. Krakauer is reluctant to leave Weathers to the care of others but Dr Caroline Mackenzie urges him to go down for his own safety.

Q 'An atmosphere of terminal entropy pervaded the camp' (p.246). How effectively does Krakauer convey the survivors' shock at the scale of the tragedy?

Q In Chapter 19 Krakauer disapprovingly cites Shigekawa's view that 8000 metres is no place for morality, yet in Chapter 20 he supports Hutchison's decision to leave Weathers and Namba. How do these cases differ?

Chapter 20: The Geneva Spur; 9.45 AM, May 12, 1996 (pp.257–64)

Summary: *Leave South Col (Camp Three); Hutchison ailing; Lopsang Jangbu distraught; arrive at Camp Two; Gau and Weathers arrive; helicopter rescue.*

Key theme: raw distress.
This chapter continues the narrative of the party's descent and describes the dramatic helicopter rescues of Gau and Weathers. Krakauer emphasises his surprise at Weathers's resilience (p.261) and his shock at the 'magnitude of this calamity' (p.264).

Q How do the Sherpas react to the tragedy? Consider Lopsang's response to Scott Fischer's death (p.260).

Q Does Krakauer's writing about the disaster and its immediate aftermath have the 'raw, ruthless sort of honesty' (p.XIII) he strove to achieve?

Chapter 21: Everest Base Camp; May 13, 1996 (pp.265–79)

Summary: *Krakauer's distress; memorial service at Base Camp; back in Seattle, Krakauer's judgement; other disasters on Everest in May 1996.*

Key theme: conclusions, yet no lessons can be drawn easily.
Krakauer attempts 'mature judgement on the expedition of a kind that was impossible when we were all up close to it' (Apsley Cherry-Garrard, *The Worst Journey in the World,* 1991, cited p.267). To do so he must put aside the raw distress, shock, grief and guilt.

Krakauer is haunted by his failure to act in the crisis and envies Klev Schoening's calm certainty that he did what he could (p.271). In his final assessment, though, Krakauer isolates the following key causes of the disaster:

- Hall's pride, or 'hubris'
- 'violent' weather is not 'extraordinary' on Everest (p.272)
- wasted time
- the rivalry between Hall and Fisher (p.273)
- hypoxia makes 'lucid thought ... impossible at 29,000 feet' (p.273)
- Nepal and China will not limit climbing because they are 'Desperate for hard currency' (p.274).

Krakauer concludes that the tragedy of May 1996 reflects the standard 1:4 ratio of risk for climbing Everest (p.274).

Epilogue: Seattle; November 29, 1996 (pp.281–8)

Summary: *Aftermath for Kasischke and Weathers; readers' responses to Krakauer's magazine article; death of Lopsang Jangbu; Boukreev injured; a Sherpa's response; Pittman criticised; Beidleman's guilt.*

Key theme: reality seems like a dream after May 1996.
Krakauer finds the safety, warmth and comfort of home in Seattle unreal. Like him, Beidleman is also wracked with guilt over having left Namba to die without turning back.

Key point

This feeling of disconnection is reflected in the fragmentary format of this chapter, which is broken up by long uninterrupted quotations documenting other people's assessments: 1) Kasischke on his recovery and his admiration of Weathers's attitude; 2) readers' scathing responses to Krakauer's journal article; 3) a Sherpa on the damage to Sherpa culture.

Q How do you interpret Charles Bowden's declaration: 'THIS IS THE REAL WORLD' (cited p.283)?

Q In the final analysis, does Krakauer judge the Everest disaster maturely?

INDIVIDUALS & RELATIONSHIPS

Jon Krakauer

Role: author of *Into Thin Air* and client on the 1996 Adventure Consultants Everest expedition

Key quotes

'But boyhood dreams die hard, I discovered, and good sense be damned ... I said yes without even pausing to catch my breath' (p.26).

'... I was a party to the death of good people, which is something that is apt to remain on my conscience for a very long time' (p.XIII).

Krakauer is a Seattle-based journalist, the author of *Into Thin Air* and a participant in the drama. In his twenties and thirties he 'lived to climb' (p.21). At 41, his 'hunger to climb had been blunted, in short, by a bunch of small satisfactions that added up to something like happiness' (p.25), but he can't resist Everest.

Krakauer is quick to judge his team-mates: he feels uncomfortable with their wealth and political outlook. However, as the expedition progresses he gains respect for them. Their shared hardship has an equalising effect, and Krakauer becomes less focused upon his fellow trekkers' political views or wealth, and more upon their humanity. He becomes uneasy about making private lives available for public consumption (p.138). He also questions whether his presence contributed to the disaster, citing Weathers's view that: "It added a lot of stress" (p.138). Much of the book is concerned with justifying his actions.

Rob Hall

Role: director of Adventure Consultants

Key quotes

'Hall's easygoing façade masked an intense desire to succeed ... and it pained him that some celebrated climbers ... didn't appreciate how difficult guiding was, or give the profession the respect he felt it deserved' (p.147).

'In a certain sense, Hall's Adventure Consultants compound served as the seat of government for the entire Base Camp, because nobody on the mountain commanded more respect than Hall' (p.60)

Hall was a 35-year-old professional mountaineer from New Zealand. Concerned that he could not climb for a living indefinitely, he and Gary Ball established Adventure Consultants. It quickly gained a reputation for safe and successful commercial expeditions, but Hall faced personal and professional challenges. In 1993 Sir Edmund Hillary publicly 'decried Hall's role in the growing commercialization of Everest' (p.34). Then Ball died of an altitude-induced cerebral oedema (p.36).

Hall had the reputation for 'the tightest, safest operation on the mountain, bar none' (p.272). He was a generous man with a good sense of humour (p.31). Hall was 'critical of some expedition leaders for being careless with their Sherpa staff' (p.53). The very moving description of Hall's final satellite telephone conversations with his friends, and his wife Jan Arnold (p.223) shows him to have been caring, thoughtful and well-loved.

Hall's controlling leadership angers Krakauer (p.167); in addition, it is an inadequate safety precaution. There are no contingency plans to cover the event that Hall is hurt or immobilised. For example, he insists that Weathers wait for him before descending, but Hall did not descend and Weathers waited for over ten hours.

Andy 'Harold' Harris

Role: Adventure Consultants guide

Key quote

'As the junior guide on Hall's team, and the only one who'd never been on Everest, Andy was eager to prove himself' (p.146).

Harris, a 31-year-old New Zealander, was an experienced climber and a junior guide for Adventure Consultants. This was his first Everest attempt. He was liked for his infectious enthusiasm, his 'laid-back' attitude (p.48) and his generosity as a guide (p.81). He contracted a stomach bug at Lobuje but refused to postpone trekking to Base Camp (p.58). He suffered from 'various intestinal ailments for most of the expedition' (p.146). In retrospect, Krakauer recognises that Harris suffered from hypoxia on the descent from Everest. He was confused and behaving strangely. When Hall radioed saying he needed help with oxygen for Hansen who had collapsed, Harris responded and, in the late afternoon of May 10, heroically climbed back up the summit ridge with two oxygen canisters. He reached Hall, but died during the night.

Mike Groom

Role: third guide hired by Adventure Consultants

Key quote

'An exceedingly calm, circumspect man, Groom was pleasant company but seldom spoke unless spoken to and replied to questions tersely, in a barely audible voice' (p.43).

Groom, a 33-year-old plumber from Brisbane, is an experienced climber and a competent guide. Krakauer praises his view that 'it would be extremely irresponsible to guide the peak without using [oxygen]' (p.154). Groom was caught in the storm with Beidleman and others, but survived.

Doug Hansen

Role: Adventure Consultants client

Key quote

'Doug was hell-bent on joining the summit push, even though his throat was still bothering him and his strength seemed to be at a low ebb' (p.148).

Hansen, a 46-year-old US postal worker, was a 'wiry, hard-partying man' (p.37) with a heart. His mountaineering had personal costs, and of his new romance he said: "I better make the summit and get Everest out of my system before she changes her mind" (p.69). This was his second Everest attempt; the year before Hall had turned him back just short of the summit. Hall offered Hansen a discounted place on this expedition.

Krakauer felt more comfortable with Hansen than the other clients. Hansen suffered frostbite and throat trouble but he remained determined. On summit day he moved slowly and at one point turned back, but continued after talking with Hall. He was late to the summit, but Hall waited. On his descent he ran out of oxygen. Hall could not move him alone, and Hansen died during the descent.

Dr Seaborn Beck Weathers

Role: Adventure Consultants client

Key quotes

"To aging Walter Mitty types like myself, Dick Bass was an inspiration ... Bass showed that Everest was within the realm of possibility for regular guys. Assuming you're reasonably fit and have some disposable income ..." (p.22).

'Beck's cheer and limitless optimism were so winning ...' (p.136).

A 49-year-old pathologist from Dallas, Weathers typifies the 'regular guy' who seeks to climb the world's highest mountain. 'Walter Mitty' is a henpecked character in James Thurber's short story 'The Secret Life of Walter Mitty' (1939), who has escapist fantasies about being a hero. Weathers developed a passion for mountaineering in his forties after taking an elementary climbing course. Climbing became an obsession, one that his wife resented (p.137). Like Bass, Weathers wanted to climb the seven summits.

At first Krakauer disliked Weathers for his political views and his 'back-slapping' humour (p.136). At other times, though, Krakauer enjoyed Weathers's 'garrulous' jokes (p.37), and during the climb he came to admire Weathers's stoicism and cheerfulness. Weathers had eye surgery shortly before the expedition, and as a side effect his vision began to fail during the ascent. Hall ordered him to wait so that they could descend together, which led to Weathers waiting in the cold for over ten hours before descending with Groom. He was then caught in the storm with the group on the South Col.

By the time Groom, Beidleman and others could see their way, Weathers was unconscious. When Boukreev rescued Pittman, Fox and Madsen, he assumed that Weathers was unable to be saved. The next day Hutchison also judged that there was no hope. Miraculously, some hours later Weathers woke up and stumbled into camp. The IMAX and Alpine Ascents teams organised a helicopter rescue.

Yasuko Namba

Role: Adventure Consultants client

Key quote

> 'Previously on the expedition she'd been a slow, uncertain climber, but today, with the summit in her crosshairs, she was energized as never before' (p.176)

Namba was a 47-year-old Japanese personnel director and an experienced climber. Krakauer characterises her as 'taciturn' (p.37) and as an 'accomplished businesswoman [who] didn't fit the meek, deferential stereotype of a middle-aged Japanese woman' (p.176). Although she had already climbed six of the seven tallest peaks in the world, her inexperience in such demanding conditions was evident. During the summit push she was so keen that she attached her jumar (fastening device) to an unsecured rope and nearly caused a disaster (p.176). During her descent from the summit, her oxygen ran out and she 'sat down, refusing to move' (p.206). Beidleman began dragging her towards Camp Four when the storm hit. By the time there was a lull in the weather, Namba was too weak to move. Later that evening Boukreev judged that she was beyond hope, and the following day Hutchison agreed.

Dr Stuart Hutchison

Role: Adventure Consultants client

Key quote

'With all our guides hors de combat, Hutchison stepped up to fill the leadership vacuum. A high-strung, self-serious young man from the upper crust of English-speaking Montreal society ... he did his best to rise to the occasion' (p.247).

A 34-year-old Canadian cardiologist, Hutchison is characterised by Krakauer as 'cerebral' (brainy) and 'wonkish' (nerdy or studious, p.37), and as 'conservative by nature' (p.177). When he learned that the summit was still three hours away, he decided to turn back. He and Taske persuaded Kasischke to join them. When Beidleman, Groom and clients returned to Camp Four at 12.45 am, Hutchison helped Groom into his tent and ascertained where Namba and Weathers were. He searched for them alone, but bad weather forced him to return (pp.212–13). He radioed Base Camp with updates (p.218) and woke Krakauer to tell him Harris was missing. He and four Sherpas found Namba and Weathers, but judged them to be almost dead and unable to be rescued (pp.247–8). On the descent from Camp Three to Camp Two, Hutchison became confused due to sheer exhaustion (pp.259–60), but arrived safely with Krakauer's assistance.

Frank Fischbeck

Role: Adventure Consultants client

Key quote

'Within three hours of leaving the Col [Camp Four], Frank decided that something about the day just didn't feel right. Stepping out of the queue, he turned around and descended to the tents' (p.165).

Fischbeck, a 53-year-old publisher from Hong Kong, is 'a dapper, genteel' man (p.37) on his fourth Everest attempt (pp.37, 54). In 1994 he turned around 330 feet below the summit (p.37); in 1996 he was the first member of the Adventure Consultants expedition to turn back. Krakauer recounts that at Camp Four, 'Frank looked as if he were in a severe state of shock, but he was doing his best to take care of Lou [Kasischke]' (p.246).

Lou Kasischke

Role: Adventure Consultants client

Key quote

'... a tall, athletic, silver-haired man with patrician reserve ...' (p.31).

Kasischke is a 53-year-old lawyer from Michigan. Like Fischbeck, Kasischke made the difficult but life-saving decision to turn back. On summit day Kasischke was 'initially reluctant to concede defeat' at 11.30 am but he was persuaded to do so (p.177). After returning to Camp Four, 'Lou was delirious and snow-blind, completely without sight, unable to do anything for himself, muttering incoherently' (p.246). Afterwards, he wrote: 'Everest was the worst experience in my life. But that was then. Now is now. I'm focusing on the positive' (p.283).

Dr John Taske

Role: Adventure Consultants client

Key quote

"When I left the military, I sort of lost my way ... My marriage fell apart. All I could see was this long dark tunnel closing in, ending in infirmity, old age, and death. Then I started to climb, and the sport provided most of what had been missing for me in civvy street – the challenge, the camaraderie, the sense of mission" (p.137).

A 57-year-old anaesthetist from Brisbane, Taske is an Australian army doctor who began climbing after retirement. He has a good sense of humour. When he realised that the summit was still three hours away and that a late arrival would jeopardise a safe return, he decided to turn around.

Ang Dorje Sherpa

Role: climbing sirdar for Adventure Consultants

Key quotes

'... bright, interested, keen to learn, and conscientious almost to a fault' (p.105).

'... Ang Dorje, standing alone in the appalling wind, sobbing inconsolably over the loss of Rob' (p.254).

Ang Dorje is Hall's head climbing Sherpa, 'a strong and resourceful climber' (p.105) who conscientiously fulfils his duties. Krakauer notes that: 'With respect and obvious affection, Hall referred to him as "my main man" and mentioned several times that he considered Ang Dorje's role crucial to the success of our expedition' (p.106). During the ascent he claimed to have 'seen ghosts in the night' and 'was not one to take such portents lightly' (p.175). He had a difficult relationship with Lopsang Jangbu, the Mountain Madness climbing sirdar (p.175). He was devastated by Hall's death: as a devout Buddhist, he '[saw] his role on this earth as keeping people safe' (p.254).

Minor figures – Adventure Consultants

Helen Wilton, Adventure Consultants Base Camp manager. This was Wilton's third season as Base Camp Manager and Krakauer describes her positively.

Dr Caroline MacKenzie, Base Camp doctor for Adventure Consultants. MacKenzie was 'an accomplished climber and physician' (p.36) who advised Krakauer to descend for his own safety rather than look after Weathers (p.256).

Chhongba Sherpa, Base Camp cook for Adventure Consultants. Chongba was a 'wry, thoughtful man' (p.47). He took Krakauer, Hansen and Kasischke to receive a blessing from the rimpoche, the head lama of Nepal (pp.47–8).

Scott Fischer

Role: mountaineer and director of Mountain Madness

Key quotes

'If the name of Hall's business, Adventure Consultants, mirrored his methodological, fastidious approach to climbing, Mountain Madness was an even more accurate reflection of Scott's personal style. By his early twenties, he had developed a reputation for a harrowing, damn-the-torpedoes approach to ascent' (p.62).

"Hey, experience is overrated. It's not the altitude that's important, it's your attitude ... We've got the big E figured out, we've got it totally wired. These days, I'm telling you, we've built a yellow brick road to the summit" (p.66).

Fischer embraced the challenge of climbing as a young man (p.63), but as a husband and father believed that he had 'become a much more careful, more conservative climber' who took fewer risks (p.65). He was tremendously likable: 'he had the kind of gregarious, magnetic personality that instantly won him friends for life' (p.63), He wanted a lucrative commercial sponsorship and public recognition, especially from his peers (p.63). By 1996 he was beginning to gain the reputation he desired but he had not quite achieved what he wanted in his life. He was striving to do better, and modelled his company Mountain Madness on Hall's Adventure Consultants. He and Hall were friends, and planned future climbs together.

Krakauer speculates that Fischer pushed ahead because he badly wanted his first commercial climb of Everest to be successful. More seriously, Krakauer criticises Fischer's lax attitude; he allowed clients to acclimatise at their own pace and did not keep track of them. During the expedition Fischer over-taxed himself by going up and down the mountain, when his head Sherpa Lopsang Jangbu became ill and again when his client Dale Kruse got HACE. He did not rest enough during his acclimatisation and failed to recognise his own limits, errors that ultimately cost Fischer his life.

Lopsang Jangbu Sherpa

Role: climbing sirdar for Mountain Madness

Key quotes

'"Mount Everest is God – for me, for everybody"
Lopsang solemnly mused …' (p.129).

'… half-crazed with grief and exhaustion … Lopsang pounded his chest and tearfully blurted, "I am very bad luck, very bad luck. Scott is dead; it is my fault. I am very bad luck. It is my fault. I am very bad luck"' (p.260).

Lopsang Sherpa is the gregarious and hard-working 23-year-old sirdar (head climbing Sherpa) for Mountain Madness (p.130). He loved working for Fischer and saw his future as being with Mountain Madness (p.131). During the Everest trek he accompanied his ailing uncle Ngawang Topche to Kathmandu and then rapidly trekked back to Base Camp. This exhausted him and compromised his acclimatisation (p.130). On summit day he further taxed himself by short-roping Sandy Pittman. He survived but was devastated to have lost Fischer.

Anatoli Boukreev

Role: Russian guide for Mountain Madness

Key quote

'The underlying problem was that Boukreev's notion of his responsibilities differed substantially from Fischer's. As a Russian, Boukreev came from a tough, proud, hardscrabble climbing culture that did not believe in coddling the weak' (p.149).

If there is a villain in *Into Thin Air*, it is Boukreev, an elite Russian mountaineer and a highly-paid guide for the Mountain Madness expedition. Krakauer devotes many pages to criticising him (see Background & Context).

Krakauer judges that Boukreev failed his duty of care towards his clients by not assisting them in the 'Death Zone' (p.210). Nevertheless, after the first group of lost climbers – Beidleman, Groom and others – returned to camp, Boukreev made a number of heroic attempts to face the raging storm, and he single-handedly rescued Pittman and Fox.

Neal Beidleman

Role: Mountain Madness guide

Key quote

'... an aerospace engineer by training, he was a quiet, thoughtful, extremely conscientious guide who was well liked ...' (p.199

Beidleman is a 36-year-old guide on his first ascent of Everest. A strong climber, he was friends with Fischer, Boukreev and Krakauer. On 10 May he knew that time was running out, but as a junior guide he was not happy to order clients to turn around. He arrived at the summit at 1.25 pm and waited for Mountain Madness clients. He descended with them and Namba at 3.10 pm. When the storm hit, Beidleman directed the group on a roundabout route to avoid a steep climb in fierce conditions. When they became lost on the South Col he waited for a clearing in the storm and then accompanied those who could walk back to camp. He was devastated by Namba's death (p.214) and *Into Thin Air* closes with the image of his haunting grief.

Sandy Hill Pittman

Role: Mountain Madness client

Key quotes

'Her tomboyishly short hair looked expertly coiffed, even here at 17,000 feet' (p.115).

'... insulated by her money, a staff of paid attendants, and unwavering self-absorption, Pittman was heedless of the resentment and scorn she inspired in others ...' (p.119).

Pittman is a reporter for NBC Interactive Media who Krakauer describes scathingly as 'a millionaire socialite-cum-climber' (p.114); he also cites an article calling her 'more ... a social climber than mountain climber' (*Wall Street Journal*, cited p.119). She luxuriated on the mountain, eating gourmet food, watching movies in her tent and reading fashion magazines delivered to Base Camp. Sherpas carried her heavy computers and solar panels from camp to camp. Krakauer is disgusted by her over-use of the Sherpas' energy. On summit day she was short-roped (pulled) by Lopsang Jangbu.

During the descent, Pittman collapsed and required an injection of dexamethasone (p.204). Lost in the storm with Beidleman and others, she became hysterical (p.208) before being rescued by Boukreev. Although Krakauer criticises her, he also acknowledges that she is modest about her climbing abilities, shares her luxuries and is cheerful.

Minor figures – Mountain Madness

Charlotte Fox, **Tim Madsen** and **Klev Schoening**, Mountain Madness clients. They were stranded on the South Col with Beidleman and others. Schoening was in the first group to return to camp, while Madsen stayed to look after Fox, his girlfriend (pp.209–10). Fox was rescued by Boukreev and Madsen followed.

Dr Ingrid Hunt, Mountain Madness doctor and Base Camp Manager. She lacked sufficient experience and mismanaged Ngawang Topche's case of HAPE (p.111).

Other key individuals

'Makalu' Gau Ming-Ho, Taiwanese expedition leader. Gau also attempted the summit on 9 May 1996. In the storm, he suffered extremely bad frostbite. He was rescued with Weathers.

Ian Woodall, South African expedition leader. Woodall was a charlatan who would not share resources with the stranded Adventure Consultants and Mountain madness teams during the crisis.

Edmund February, South African expedition member. February spoke to Krakauer about Woodall's dishonesty.

David Breashears and Ed Viesturs, IMAX team. Breashears (director and professional climber) provided oxygen to the stranded climbers. He and Viesturs (professional climber starring in the IMAX film) rescued Weathers and Gau.

THEMES, IDEAS & VALUES

Storytelling

Key quotes

'We tell ourselves stories in order to live ... We look for the sermon in the suicide, for the social or moral lesson in the murder ... We live entirely, especially if we are writers, by the imposition of a narrative line upon disparate images, by the "ideas" with which we have learned to freeze the shifting phantasmagoria which is our actual experience' (Joan Didion, cited p.123).

'The slopes of Everest did not lack for dreamers in the spring of 1996 ... Everest has always been a magnet for kooks, publicity seekers, hopeless romantics, and others with a shaky hold on reality' (pp.87–8).

At a number of places, Krakauer signals that conventions of fiction writing help him to make sense of the real events upon which *Into Thin Air* is based. Perhaps this is most obvious in the opening of the book. Krakauer calls the list of people (and expeditions) on Mount Everest in May 1996 '*Dramatis Personæ*' (pp.XVII–XXII). This literary term is usually used to describe the characters in a play, and yet *Into Thin Air* is about real people and real events.

This suggestion of a slip between fiction and reality is extended on the following page by the words of Spanish philosopher, José Ortega y Gasset: 'Men play at tragedy because they do not believe in the reality of the tragedy which is actually being staged in the civilised world' (cited p.XXIII). By opening the book with these words, Krakauer implies that the people involved in the Everest disaster did not recognise that they were playing roles in a tragedy on the world stage. They did not foresee that disaster was going to strike them, and they did not really believe it could strike. For this reason they did not safeguard their lives vigilantly enough.

In addition, they could not anticipate that a disaster would throw them into the public eye, where their motives, characters and decisions would be scrutinised. *Into Thin Air* is the natural result of this process, an attempt to make a narrative out of the disaster in order to keep going. As Didion says: 'We tell ourselves stories to live ... We live ... by the imposition of a narrative line upon ... our actual experience'.

Tragic drama

The opening allusions to *dramatis personæ* and tragedy suggest that tragic drama is the 'narrative line' Krakauer imposes upon the chaos of 'actual experience' in order to derive a 'social or moral lesson'. These are not the only references to tragedy. Krakauer describes Hall's profound self-reliance as 'Hubris' (p.272). This is an Ancient Greek term meaning pride. It is conventionally applied to tragic heroes in Greek drama (such as Sophocles' *King Oedipus*) or epic (Homer's *The Odyssey*, for instance). Hubris is a kind of extreme self-confidence that leads heroes to blindly disregard the gods and thus make tragedy inevitable.

By using this term, Krakauer implies that Hall's overblown sense of his own strength and resilience is his fatal flaw. Krakauer suggests that Hall is larger than life, a kind of monumental figure who, like a Greek hero, towers above the rest of humanity but who has further to fall when his fortune turns. Krakauer draws the reader's attention to the fictional devices he uses to construct the story he is telling about real events.

The story's message

Concluding *Into Thin Air*, Krakauer clarifies what he did *not* try to achieve:

> to believe that dissecting the tragic events of 1996 in minute detail will actually reduce the future death rate in any meaningful way is wishful thinking ... If you can convince yourself that Rob Hall died because he made a string of stupid errors and that you are too clever to repeat those same errors, it makes it easier for you to attempt Everest in the face of some rather compelling evidence that doing so is injudicious [unwise]. (p.274)

The social and moral message Krakauer extracts from the disaster is not a straightforward lesson of what not to do when climbing Everest. In fact he thinks armchair diagnosis of the problem is dangerous: it could indirectly encourage others to face the very same dangers believing that they have learned the crucial lessons. Nevertheless, Krakauer does have a lesson to teach his readers; he does believe that 'We tell ourselves stories to live'. His story attempts to strip back the 'romantic scrim' (p.44) that blinds men to the realities of high-altitude climbing.

Key point

Into Thin Air is a story created out of the chaos of tragic experience, in order to revise attitudes towards mountaineering.

Krakauer feels that traditional romantic adventure or quest stories about mountaineering idealise risk. Such stories propel individuals, particularly men, to embrace mountaineering and thus blithely participate in a drama inevitably driven towards tragedy. Krakauer suggests that some stories (from fiction and nonfiction) prepare people with a vision, plot or 'dream' which prevents them from seeing reality for what it is. He describes the English climber George Leigh Mallory in the following terms:

> A product of upper-tier English society, [Mallory] was also an aesthete and idealist with decidedly romantic sensibilities ... While tent-bound high on Everest, Mallory and his companions would read aloud to one another from *Hamlet* and *King Lear* (p.16).

The word 'romantic' is important here: for Krakauer this aesthetic attitude entails blindness. The fact that Mallory read great tragedies while on the slopes of Mount Everest seems no accident, since Mallory's own noble quest of ascending the world's highest peak ended in his tragic death. Mallory's 'romantic sensibilities' were produced by the literature he read. It would be going too far to say that reading Shakespearean tragedy actually caused Mallory's own tragic death, but Krakauer is concerned to identify what makes men glorify risk and climb mountains.

Reality versus the dream

Key quote

'Straddling the top of the world, one foot in China and the other in Nepal, I cleared the ice from my oxygen mask, hunched a shoulder against the wind, and stared absently down at the vastness of Tibet ... I'd been fantasizing about this moment, and the release of emotion that would accompany it, for many months. But now that I was finally here, actually standing on the summit of Mount Everest, I just couldn't summon the energy to care' (p.5).

Krakauer describes the ethos of mountaineering as 'romantic' or 'a dream'. He is not alone in identifying its source in books. In *Everest: The West Ridge*, Thomas F. Hornbein recalls a 'blurred' black and white photograph:

> Everest itself, sitting back from the front ones, didn't even appear highest, but it didn't matter. It was; the legend said so. Dreams were the key to the picture, permitting a boy to enter it, to stand at the crest of the windswept ridge, to climb toward the summit ... (cited on p.13)

As a climber, Krakauer shared this dream but the devastating experience of May 1996 has left him disillusioned.

Krakauer's long-harboured dream does not match the reality he experiences: this is his social or cultural lesson. Standing on top of Mount Everest is not the heroic achievement he had imagined it would be. In addition, the descent involved the devastating loss of many lives.

Masculinity and climbing

Key quote

'[Everest] was one of those uninhibited dreams that come free with growing up. I was sure that mine about Everest was not mine alone; the highest point on earth, unattainable, foreign to all experience, was there for many boys and grown men to aspire toward' (Hornbein, cited on p.13).

The dream of climbing Everest is tied to certain ideals of masculinity. In this idealised view, climbing Everest leads a man to embrace adventure, visit an exotic land and embark on an extremely dangerous journey. He thus achieves insight and glory, becoming a hero if he survives the baptism of fire and achieves the object of his quest. Boiled down to this, the quest for Everest echoes mythical quests for the Holy Grail, or King Arthur's sword Excalibur. Just as mythical quests involve brave knights in shining armour, so too the Everest quest confers glory upon the brave and valiant man who reaches the highest peak in the world.

This fantasy, dream or romantic vision is instilled in boyhood. Like so many other boys, Krakauer 'dreamed of ascending Everest' (p.20). He draws upon his own experience to describe what it means to grow into this dream. The fantasy led to a way of life as a young man. He reflects:

> To become a climber was to join a self-contained, rabidly idealistic society, largely unnoticed and surprisingly uncorrupted by the world at large. The culture of ascent was characterized by intense competition and undiluted machismo ... (p.20)

Climbing culture is based upon competitive masculine ideals, which fuel climbers to take risks in order to achieve glory. The Everest expedition makes Krakauer reconsider these ideals.

Questioning the masculine ideals

During the expedition Krakauer questions Hall's acclimatisation plan:

> "It's worked thirty-nine times so far, pal," Hall assured me with a crooked grin when I confessed my doubts. "And a few of the blokes who've summitted with me were nearly as pathetic as you." (p.70)

Hall uses the rhetoric of manly bravado ('pal', 'blokes') and the good-humoured put-down joke ('nearly as pathetic as you') to bolster his authority.

Hall encourages Krakauer to disregard his own instincts. He does the same when Hansen worries about his health during the climb:

> "Don't write yourself off just yet, Douglas," Rob offered. "Wait and see how you feel in a couple of days. You're a tough bastard. I think you've still got a good shot at the top once you recover." (p.125)

These jokes are competitive machismo in action. Hall appeals to Krakauer and Hansen's manliness – "You're a tough bastard", or through the implied question 'you are not really as pathetic as you seem, are you?' – in order to encourage them to keep climbing to his plan.

Into Thin Air is not a tale about heroic manhood vindicated (justified). Krakauer recognises bitterly that he is not a hero in this quest. His manhood is not confirmed and strengthened through his Everest adventure; rather, he feels emasculated.

- Oxygen deprivation weakens him. He tries to help the Sherpas to make a platform in the ice for a tent at Camp Four: 'At 24,000 feet, I could manage only seven or eight blows of my ice ax before having to pause for more than a minute to catch my breath. My contribution to the effort was negligible' (p.139).
- He depends on the work of others. Chopping ice for three hours to make drinking water for his fellow climbers 'gave me a fresh perspective on how much the Sherpas ordinarily did for us, and how little we truly appreciated it' (p.151).
- His independent judgement is strictly limited by Hall.
- He does not act heroically in the crisis (although Boukreev, Hutchison, Beidleman and the Sherpas do); he only saves himself.
- As a client he is 'indoctrinated' (p.188) to be passive. Consequently he fails to notice that Harris, his team-mate and guide, is suffering from hypoxia, and to offer Harris assistance.

Krakauer is not telling this story in order to mourn the breakdown of his own manhood, rather he is trying to tell the Everest story as it was. The truth is that myths of masculinity do not match reality.

Risk and mountaineering

Key quote

'I'd always known that climbing mountains was a high-risk pursuit ... Until I visited the Himalaya, however, I'd never actually seen death at close range ... Mortality had remained a conveniently hypothetical concept, an idea to ponder in the abstract ... the shock was magnified by the sheer superfluity of the carnage' (p.270–1).

Key quote

'It was as if there were an unspoken agreement on the mountain to pretend that these desiccated remains weren't real – as if none of us dared to acknowledge what was at stake here' (p.107).

When Krakauer observes that mountaineering 'is an activity that idealizes risk-taking' (p.275), he indicates his own shifting perspective on that risk. Although the glory of climbing depends upon the climber's preparedness to risk and survive risk, Krakauer comes to believe that mountaineering culture does not fully apprehend risk. Krakauer is a seasoned climber, yet he was not prepared for Everest. During the ascent, Krakauer is particularly shocked to see the frozen bodies of climbers who died on their Everest quest.

In addition, Krakauer comes to understand risk-taking in moral and cultural terms. For example, the clients choose to take the risk of climbing Everest. Indeed, 'The possibility of danger serves merely to sharpen [the climber's] awareness and control' (Alvarez, cited p.73); risk is integral to the sport. However, when clients push to reach the summit in the face of their own ailing physical and mental health and then cannot manage to descend unassisted, they place team-members and guides at risk.

Krakauer also believes that group members have different responsibilities in relationship to risk. For example, guides and leaders should minimise risk for their clients, and this may involve making the hard decision to turn back in order to minimise risk. He also sees that the Sherpas have a different relationship to risk from the amateur and professional climbers.

Sherpas and mountaineering

Key quote

'Sherpas remain an enigma to most foreigners, who tend to regard them through a romantic scrim' (p.44).

Although some Westerners might feel that being served by Sherpas on an expedition adds to the romance of mountaineering in the Himalayas, Krakauer feels uneasy about it. During the trek he wears a Buddhist talisman, 'a Xistone' (p.126), blessed by the lama. This signals his desire to respect local traditions. Throughout his narrative, Krakauer tries to strip back the 'romantic scrim' and look at the Sherpas honestly.

The 'romantic scrim'

Krakauer describes the stunning features of the landscape in highly poetic language: 'the crepuscular gorge of the Dudh Kosi' (p.41); 'a glaze of frost sparkled from the rhododendron leaves' (p.41); 'aromatic stands of pine' (p.42); 'spectacularly fluted ice pinnacles of Thamserku and Kusum Kangru' (p.42); 'the Valkyrian skyline bristled with peaks' (p.48). These phrases emphasise the overwhelming beauty of the landscape.

The description 'Valkyrian skyline' is part of the 'romantic scrim' through which Westerners look at mountains. In old Norse mythology the Valkyrie are twelve handmaidens chosen by the god Odin to select the most heroic men slain in battle and take them to Valhalla. Nineteenth-century Romantic art and culture popularised this myth, particularly the operas of Richard Wagner (1813–83).

Krakauer stresses that this landscape has hundreds of years of human history, that of the mountain-dwelling Sherpa people. Poetic terms – the Western vocabulary for describing mountains – create a warped perspective through which Westerners view Mount Everest. Krakauer suggests that such language highlights the beauty, or aesthetic qualities, of the physical landscape at the expense of the cultural or human dimensions.

Krakauer attempts to shatter this illusion by:

- offering a thick description of Sherpa life on the slopes of the mountain
- mentioning Sherpa beliefs and customs where relevant
- describing in a critical tone the Westerner who patronises a Sherpani by speaking to her in pidgin English, assuming that she is ill-educated and ignorant (pp.43–4)
- giving a history of Sherpa culture
- describing his visit to the monastery at Tengboche for a blessing from a Buddhist Lama (pp.47–8)
- outlining impacts of Western culture on the Sherpas – the positives of improved health services, education and jobs, are pitted against the negatives of exploitation, degradation and filth (particularly of the toilets and flea-infested lodges)
- citing Hall's reminder that the expedition relies upon Sherpas (p.53).

For international mountaineers, climbing is a form of recreation; the activity itself is not necessary but the rewards – experience and insight – make it worthwhile. By contrast, the Sherpas' primary motivation for climbing is their livelihood. They may want fame, but only to guarantee future work. Therefore, mountaineers and Sherpas have a very different relationship to the risks involved: for the mountaineers, risk makes a climb exhilarating and noble, but 'for the Sherpas there is nothing noble about the risk at all; there is only a kind of threat that must be managed, negotiated ... mountaineering is simply the best-paying way to support ordinary life' (Ortner 1997, p.140).

Evolving nature of Sherpa culture

Key quotes

'Longtime visitors to the Khumbu are saddened by the boom in tourism and the change it has wrought on what early Western climbers regarded as an earthly paradise ... The transformation of the Khumbu culture is certainly not all for the best, but I didn't hear many Sherpas bemoaning the changes' (pp.45–6).

'It seems more than a little patronizing for Westerners to lament the loss of the good old days when life in the Khumbu was so much simpler and more picturesque. Most of the people who live in this rugged country seem to have no desire to be severed from the modern world or the untidy flow of human progress' (p.46).

Krakauer identifies the Western nostalgia for the now lost authentic Sherpa culture as part of the 'romantic scrim' (p.44), related to the persistent fantasy of a 'real-life Shangri-La' (p.45; Shangri-La is a mythical Tibetan paradise described in James Hilton's 1933 novel, *Lost Horizon*). In reality, Sherpa culture is constantly evolving, and teenagers are 'more likely to be wearing jeans and Chicago Bulls T-shirts than quaint traditional robes' (p.45).

Krakauer reiterates this message when he describes his own visit to the Buddhist monastery at Tengboche for a blessing by the lama. Since he makes it clear elsewhere that he views Buddhist beliefs as superstition, his visit to the lama must be understood as one of respect. Krakauer is surprised when His Holiness talks of his own visit to America rather than sacred things (p.48). Such examples show the intercultural reality of Himalayan life for Sherpas and climbers alike.

Krakauer's response

Krakauer approves that 'Buddhism as practiced by the Sherpas was a refreshingly supple and nondogmatic religion' (p.129). Here Krakauer praises the Sherpas' 'refreshing' flexibility because it allows him to be flexible in his own approach to their views, and he does not feel the need to be dogmatic in respecting Buddhist superstition himself while on Everest.

At a number of points, Krakauer records the Sherpas' sense that the goddess of the mountain is unhappy. For example, the Sherpas see Ngawang Topche's illness as evidence that 'one of the climbers in Fischer's team had angered Everest – Sagarmatha, goddess of the sky – and the deity had taken her revenge' (p.127). Krakauer records their point of view and discusses its 'animistic' character (that is, it attributes human characteristics to inanimate objects, like the mountain), but he does not seriously consider whether it has any bearing on the tragic events.

Values: the ethics of climbing

Key quotes

'In climbing, having confidence in your partners is no small concern. One climber's actions can affect the welfare of the entire team' (p.37).

'... the most rewarding aspects of mountaineering derive from the sport's emphasis on self-reliance, making critical decisions and dealing with the consequences, on personal responsibility. When you sign on as a client, I discovered, you are forced to give up all that, and more' (pp.167–8).

As a counter to Shigekawa's attitude that "Above 8,000 meters is not a place where people can afford morality" (p.241), Krakauer provides a number of examples of ethical actions at altitude:

- In 1992 Scott Fischer, Ed Viesturs and others 'encountered Hall struggling to cope with a barely conscious Ball ... unable to move under his own power. [They] helped drag Ball down the avalanche-swept lower slopes of the mountain through the blizzard, saving his life' (pp.61–2).
- In 1953 Pete Schoening and his team were caught in a blizzard, waiting to attempt to summit K2. When a member developed 'thrombophlebitis, a life-threatening altitude-induced blood clot', the team abandoned its summit goal and 'started lowering him down' (p.91). In the process, one climber slipped, pulling four others with him, but 'Reflexively wrapping the rope around his shoulders and ice ax, Schoening somehow managed to single-handedly ... arrest the slide of the five falling climbers' (p.91).

These heroic stories are drawn from professional climbing expeditions, in which the members of a team rely upon one another. Team-members' fates are intertwined literally by the rope that links them to the other climbers. This is the environment in which Krakauer has climbed in the past.

Ethics and commercial climbing

Key quotes

'... trust in one's partners is a luxury denied those who sign on as clients on a guided ascent; one must put one's faith in the guide instead' (p.38).

'My inability to discern the obvious was exacerbated to some degree by the guide-client protocol ... we had been specifically indoctrinated not to question our guides' judgment' (p.188).

Krakauer implies that the newly emerging commercial environment of Everest adventure tourism requires a different ethical code. Climbers are not roped to one another but their fates are nonetheless tied. If a client over-taxes him or herself, or over-taxes the energies of leaders, guides or Sherpas, this has consequences for other group members. This is not necessarily an immoral or selfish act; it could simply be a matter of inexperience. A client inexperienced at altitude cannot accurately calculate the risks or consequences of their action or inaction.

By necessity this places the greater burden of moral responsibility on the guides, and particularly the group leader. The leader must assess the risks and consequences for the whole party. The guides must do everything they can to enhance their ability to assist their clients.

Difficult moral choices

Key quote

'My actions – or failure to act – played a direct role in the death of Andy Harris ... The stain this has left on my psyche is not the sort of thing that washes off after a few months of grief and guilt-ridden self-reproach' (p.271).

Krakauer feels remorse over his own behaviour on Everest in May 1996. Although he cannot get over his guilt, he reassures himself and his readers that he could do no more in the circumstances because he was exhausted, 'indoctrinated' not to exercise his better judgement, and hypoxic and therefore unable to recognise the unfolding situation or think decisively about it.

In this situation we could say that, like others on the mountain, Krakauer has moral responsibilities to:

- himself and those at home (particularly those who depend upon him, such as his wife)
- team-members
- strangers on the mountain.

In determining his course of action, a climber must balance these obligations against one another and sometimes prioritise some over others. The moving account of Hall's final telephone call with his wife is a poignant reminder that in fulfilling what he considered his ethical responsibility to his client – to stay with Hansen when he was ailing, and then dying, high on the mountain – Hall relinquished his responsibility to his wife and unborn child.

Here Krakauer is struggling with heroic ideals he fails to live up to. There is a distinction between what he should do, and heroism – that is, what it would be good to do but not wrong not to do. Although others did manage to act heroically in the circumstances and they are admirable for doing so, a person does not have a moral obligation to be a hero.

The extremity of the situation on Everest meant that there were no clear-cut correct moral choices. It was a matter of weighing up imperfect moral options. For example, when Beidleman decided to take those who could move back to Camp Four during the lull in the storm, he left behind Namba and Weathers who could not move. His decision was guided by the principle of the greater good: by taking those who were fit he hoped to save some of them and to organise help for those still stranded. If they had all stayed, they might have all died.

Although Beidleman made the best decision he could under the circumstances, he remained tortured by the human cost of that decision. By closing *Into Thin Air* with Beidleman's words – "I can still feel [Yasuko Namba's] fingers sliding across my biceps, and then letting go. I never even turned to look back" (p.288) – Krakauer drives home the message that there are no easy ethical decisions in situations as extreme as the 1996 Everest disaster.

DIFFERENT INTERPRETATIONS

Different interpretations arise from different responses to a text. There is no single correct reading or interpretation of a text. However, an interpretation is more than an 'opinion' – it is the justification of a point of view on the text as a whole or on one element of it. To present an interpretation of the text based on your point of view you must use a logical argument and relevant evidence from the text to support and strengthen it.

Into Thin Air can be viewed from many different angles. Indeed the book encourages viewers to come to their own point of view about the disastrous events on Mount Everest in May 1996. It also raises a number of controversial issues that are bound to produce divided responses in readers. For example:

- the ethical question of when it is right to leave a person to die on the mountain
- the commercial question of whether any price is high enough to pay someone to risk their life to ensure a client's safety
- the related question of whether it is ethical to guide amateurs into a situation for which they are ill-prepared, and therefore unable to assess accurately the best course of action in the case of a disaster
- the cultural question of whether the presence of international climbers in the Khumbu region has improved or ruined Sherpa culture
- the question of whether Krakauer's personal guilt is justified – did he fail his co-climbers on Everest in May 1996?

In developing an interpretation of a text, it is useful to identify what the author says they are striving to achieve, and then measure what you see in the text against this. Decide for yourself whether you think the author achieves their stated goal.

Sometimes a text does not quite match what the author says about it. There are many reasons for this: the author may have other unconscious motives for writing; the author may have shifted their own point of view on the text over time; or the author may be trying to deflect criticism. In any case, it is useful to be aware of whether your own interpretation goes *with* the grain of the book – that is, accepts the author's account of it – or whether your interpretation goes *against* the grain, regarding what the author says about it with suspicion or questioning whether it is as open-minded as the author thinks it is.

The role of the preface

These are useful things to consider in relation to *Into Thin Air* because Krakauer does lay out his intentions clearly in the Preface. He also clarifies what he hopes to achieve at a number of places in the body of the book, for example when he discusses the power of the boyhood Everest dream in order to dismantle that dream and diminish its power, or where he questions the ethics of journalism, namely his own public reporting of private lives and intimate experiences for all to judge.

The following sections demonstrate two different interpretations of *Into Thin Air*, one that goes with the grain of the text and another that goes against the grain.

Interpretation 1

In *Into Thin Air* Jon Krakauer successfully uses his own personal experience to make the tragic events described seem real.

This point of view accepts Krakauer's project at face value. To justify this interpretation:

- consider the points where Krakauer talks about his deliberate use of the personal narrative style. For example, discuss his statement in the Preface: 'I wanted my account to have a raw, ruthless sort of honesty that seemed in danger of leaching away with the passage of time and the dissipation of anguish' (p.XIII).
- examine key scenes or topics where Krakauer brings in his personal history and his own experiences on the 1996 Everest expedition. This discussion will demonstrate how the author's personal experience enhances his account of these scenes or topics.

Textual evidence

Krakauer's personal experience of the Everest expedition is conveyed by his descriptions of his feelings about arriving at the summit, or about being a passive client in a commercial expedition, or his experience of altitude sickness. These experiences allow Krakauer to approach a topic from the inside, drawing on the authority of his own experience and then moving away to use that experience as a starting point for understanding other people's experiences. His description of the discomfort caused by his own mild altitude sickness (p.67) gives the reader a measure against which to consider the cases of severe altitude sickness.

He also draws on personal experience in putting forward his position in the debate about supplemental oxygen. He gives a history of the use of oxygen to assist high-altitude climbing, and also of the opposing position held by those who consider it 'aesthetically preferable' (p.154) to forgo supplemental oxygen. He criticises guides like Boukreev for not using it, and then he adds his own experience: 'Climbing along the blade of the summit ridge, sucking gas into my ragged lungs, I enjoyed a strange, unwarranted sense of calm' (p.179). Here Krakauer draws on his own experience to add a detail that is missing from other hard, factual accounts.

Krakauer often draws on his prior experiences to enhance the background information he provides on a topic. For example, he does this when discussing how a boyhood dream can become a way of life, and how the values enshrined in the myths of adventure and quest come to underpin the competitive machismo of climbing culture. He also draws on his own experience of climbing culture as a measure against which to assess the relationships between members of commercial expeditions. Finally, Krakauer uses his prior climbing experience as a reference point for describing the specific challenge of climbing Everest: 'Ascending Everest is a long, tedious process, more like a mammoth construction project than climbing as I'd previously known it' (p.73).

Interpretation 2

***Into Thin Air* fails to address adequately anything but the author's own personal struggle.**

This point of view judges that Krakauer's use of the personal narrative does not succeed. In order to substantiate this interpretation:

- re-examine Krakauer's statement about his raw honest narrative style and mount a case that goes against the grain
- analyse examples of where Krakauer fails to see beyond his own experience of an event, or where he too readily uses his prior history to explain other people's experience.

Textual evidence

Krakauer fails to see beyond his own experience in cases where he assumes that he has enough evidence upon which to base a judgement. This occurs in many different places in the text, such as when he judges that Weathers must be in pain with his new boots although he is not complaining.

The more controversial points are where Krakauer makes a moral judgement of another person's behaviour or decisions, such as his view that Boukreev is a selfish guide. In making this judgement he assumes that he has enough information, based on what he has observed and what other expedition members have told him, to justify his point of view, and to warrant making it public in his book. Whereas Krakauer admits that what he can conclude of Hall's motivations in his last hours 'is highly speculative' (p.230), at no point does Krakauer concede that there is also an element of speculation in his conclusions about Boukreev. Krakauer is not even-handed here. He gives the benefit of the doubt to Hall, since he knew and liked him as a person, but he does not do so for Boukreev, whom he did not know so well and did not immediately like.

Krakauer admits that even with his significant prior experience he is unable to explain the 1996 Everest disaster. He acknowledges that although he was an experienced climber, until this point 'Mortality had remained a conveniently hypothetical concept' (p.271). That is, nothing in his experience prepared him for the reality of the disaster. He also frequently writes about his inability to grasp the extent of the disaster: 'The magnitude of this calamity was so far beyond anything I'd ever imagined that my brain simply shorted out and went dark' (p.264).

QUESTIONS & ANSWERS

The essay topics below show a range of possible styles and formats, and are suitable for senior English assessment tasks and examinations.

Essay topics

1 "My intent … was to tell what happened on the mountain as accurately and honestly as possible, and to do so in a sensitive, respectful manner." (p.289)
Does Jon Krakauer achieve this in *Into Thin Air*?
(Consider how the author's stated objectives shape the text, then assess whether they are achieved.)

2 *Into Thin Air* is a powerful 'personal account of the Everest disaster', but how successfully does it tell the other participants' stories?
(Consider what the first-person narrative includes and excludes from the story.)

3 "I'd been fantasizing about this moment … for many months. But now that I was finally here, actually standing on the summit of Mount Everest, I just couldn't summon the energy to care." (p.5)
Why does Krakauer find the achievement of his dream anticlimactic?
(Consider how the text explores the key idea that dreams motivate climbers, and that reality can be a disappointment.)

4 Shigekawa states: "We were too tired to help. Above 8,000 meters is not a place where people can afford morality." (p.241)
Is this Krakauer's position in *Into Thin Air*?
(Consider the moral argument presented in the text.)

5 "Sherpas remain an enigma to most foreigners, who tend to regard them through a romantic scrim." (p.44)
Does Krakauer succeed in presenting the Sherpas differently?
(Consider how the text presents viewpoints on the Sherpas and their culture.)

6 "The fact that a climber has paid a large sum of money to join a guided expedition does not, by itself, mean that he or she is unfit to be on the mountain." (p.90)
How sympathetic is Krakauer to the commercialisation of Mount Everest?

(Consider the author's views of the people and situations he describes.)

7 How important is the relationship between Fischer and Hall in this text? (Assess the significance of a key relationship.)

8 '*Into Thin Air* turns the chaos of a real disaster into a black-and-white morality tale where Hall is the hero and Boukreev the villain.' Discuss.

(Consider how Krakauer uses techniques such as plot construction and characterisation to draw the reader's attention to ethical and moral questions.)

9 *Into Thin Air* weaves together different eyewitness accounts to establish the story of what exactly happened. How well does the description 'a personal account' fit this book?

(Consider the different narrative techniques employed in this multi-layered text.)

10 '*Into Thin Air* explores the boyhood dream that inspires men to climb mountains, but it throws little light on what motivates women to climb.' Discuss.

(Consider whether the text has a gender bias; this is an issue which will generate different interpretations.)

11 '*Into Thin Air* shows that when people's lives are threatened their main priority is their own survival.'
Discuss.

(Consider the text's view on how the individuals respond to the crisis.)

Analysing a sample topic

10. *Into Thin Air* explores the boyhood dream that inspires men to climb mountains, but it throws little light on what motivates women to climb.' Discuss.

First, identify the **key terms:** 'boyhood dream' and 'motivates women'.

Then, identify the **implication of the topic:** that *Into Thin Air* successfully explains why men climb but says little about women. The assumption is that it should say something about both.

What is your response? Do you **agree, disagree, partially agree or partially disagree**? For the purposes of this exercise, let's agree that *Into Thin*

Air does successfully explain the dream that inspires men to climb, and argue that it does briefly discuss why women climb and also complicates the issue by discussing why Sherpas climb.

Evidence and main points

Justify your position with examples from the text:

- picture books inspire the dream in boys
- climbing involves masculine heroic ideals
- Sandy Hill Pittman and her father
- Lopsang Jangbu or Ang Dorje.

Arrange points thematically into three or four headings and make notes.

- Why men from the West climb and what inspires them to do so, e.g.
    - o books, the dream, heroic masculine ideals and risk taking
    - o Krakauer's own boyhood and young adulthood and climbing.
- Why women climb, e.g.
    - o Sandy Hill Pittman – her father introduced her to the outdoors and climbing
    - o Pittman's climb is widely publicised so fame may be one explanation.
- Why Sherpas climb, e.g.
    - o livelihood, necessary to take the risk for that reason
    - o for fame, perhaps, but fame guarantees work.

Write the introduction

Jon Krakauer's *Into Thin Air* does give a thorough analysis of the books that stimulate the dream that inspires men from affluent first-world countries to embrace climbing in spite of the risks. He also gives a thorough description of the ethos of competitive machismo sustained within climbing culture. However, this is not just a book about why boys and men dream about climbing mountains; Krakauer offers a more complex and varied picture than that. Through the example of Sandy Hill Pittman he gives some insight into why women climb. He also offers a cultural analysis of the very different reasons that motivate Sherpas to climb. Whereas women like Pittman climb for some of the same reasons as first-world men, such as fame and adventure, Sherpas climb for their livelihood.

SAMPLE ANSWER

6. "The fact that a climber has paid a large sum of money to join a guided expedition does not, by itself, mean that he or she is unfit to be on the mountain." How sympathetic is Krakauer to the commercialisation of Mount Everest?

Jon Krakauer was commissioned by *Outside* magazine to write a feature article on the commercialisation of Mount Everest focusing on the new era of extreme adventure tourism. Following the first ascent by an amateur climber (Dick Bass) in 1985, hundreds of other 'marginally qualified dreamers' sought to realise their Everest aspirations by paying for a place on a guided expedition. This was Krakauer's brief, but the experience proved disastrous and he found it more difficult to judge than he had anticipated. The experience changed Krakauer and led him to reconsider the ethics of guiding non-professional climbers on Everest.

Krakauer begins his Everest trip as someone who readily judges others. He makes immediate judgements of them, often based upon their wealth. He is uncomfortable about the wealth of other Adventure Consultants clients. When the first group dinner is dominated by Beck Weathers's right-wing politics and 'back-slapping humour', Krakauer makes a judgement about the group and withdraws. He observes that he felt more comfortable with Doug Hansen because, like Krakauer, he was not a wealthy man. Krakauer's scathing description of the luxuries millionaire socialite Sandy Hill Pittman takes to Everest is very unsympathetic. If it isn't wealth that makes these people unfit for the mountain, then it's their attitudes, and those attitudes seem to go hand-in-hand with wealth. For example, Pittman has Sherpas waiting on her, and this insulates her from the hardship of the mountain and blinds her to her own impact on others. Krakauer's early assessments of clients do reveal his own prejudice towards wealthy people on Everest.

During the expedition, though, Krakauer notes that his attitudes have shifted. Somehow the shared 'toil, tedium, and suffering' of the high-altitude expedition brings him to see some of his wealthy team-mates in different terms. For example, he comes to admire Weathers for his stoicism. Weathers does not complain when 'his inflexible new boots had chewed his feet into hamburger' (p.136); he remains infectiously cheerful. Krakauer becomes more sympathetic to Kasischke and Taske when he learns of their dedication to climbing and their struggle to achieve their goals. When Krakauer glimpses a human dimension, he is less judgemental of these wealthy men. He can see that in their own way they have struggled for their right to be on the mountain.

Krakauer's attitude towards Pittman, however, does not change; it remains unforgiving. He condemns her for the burden she places on others, particularly the Sherpas assisting her. Pittman is in the Mountain Madness expedition, so Krakauer does not have the same opportunity to revise his initial judgements. Nevertheless, the fact that he revises his judgement of Weathers and others does not make him more cautious in judging other wealthy amateurs just because they are wealthy. At one point he explains that, because Pittman had solicited media attention, she was fair game for his journalistic scrutiny. It is fair to conclude that although Krakauer thinks he is being balanced in saying that wealth does not make people unfit to be on the mountain, he does maintain a prejudiced attitude.

Krakauer comes to see that in buying a place in a guided expedition, wealthy clients pay others for their judgement and expertise. In other words, they abdicate personal responsibility to their guides and leaders. The problem isn't exactly that they have the spare $65 000 to do this, but that 'climbing Everest has always been an extraordinarily dangerous undertaking and doubtless always would be'. The issue of whether wealthy clients are fit or 'unfit to be on the mountain' is less important than recognising the fact that in the Death Zone 'the strongest guides in the world are sometimes powerless to save even their own lives' (p.275).

REFERENCES & READING

Text

Krakauer, Jon 1997, *Into Thin Air: A Personal Account of the Everest Disaster,* Pan Macmillan, London.

Film

Into Thin Air: Death on Everest 1997, dir. Robert Markowitz, Sony Pictures. Starring Peter Horton, Nat Parker, Richard Jenkins and Christopher McDonald.

Websites

Jon Krakauer 1996, 'Into Thin Air', http://outside.away.com/outside/destinations/199609/199609_into_thin_air_1.html

Krakauer's original journal article on the fateful 1996 ascent of Everest. His book is an expanded and emended version of this article.

http://www.adventureconsultants.co.nz

This is the website of the company established by Rob Hall.

http://news.bbc.co.uk/2/hi/uk_news/magazine/5016536.stm

This is a BBC news report about a man left to die on Everest: 40 climbers passed him and did not aid him. There is a very interesting record of readers' debate.

http://classic.mountainzone.com/climbing/fischer/index.html

http://www.pbs.org/wgbh/nova/everest/

http://www.everestnews.com/everest2006/coupleeverest2006dis05292006.htm

http://channel.nationalgeographic.com/channel/highspeed/everest/

This website offers an interactive virtual climbing tour of Mount Everest.

http://www.spj.org/ethicscode.asp

The code of journalistic ethics provided on the (US) Society of Professional Journalists homepage.

Background reading

Bayers, Peter L. 2003, *Imperial Ascent: Mountaineering, Masculinity, and Empire*, University Press of Colorado, Boulder.

Boukreev, Anatoli and G. Weston DeWalt 1997, *The Climb: Tragic Ambitions on Everest*, St Martin's Press, New York.

Breashears, David 1999, *High Exposure: An Enduring Passion for Everest and Unforgiving Places,* Simon & Schuster, New York.

Kayes, D. Christopher 2002, 'Dilemma at 29,000 feet: an exercise in ethical decision making based on the Mt. Everest climbing disaster', *Journal of Management Education*, vol. 26, no. 3, pp.307–21.

Kayes, D. Christopher 2004, 'The 1996 Mount Everest climbing disaster: the breakdown of learning in teams', *Human Relations,* vol. 57, no. 10, pp.1263–84.

Nicolson, Marjorie Hope 1959, *Mountain Gloom and Mountain Glory: The Development of the Aesthetics of the Infinite,* Cornell University Press, Ithaca, New York.

Ortner, Sherry B. 1997, 'Thick resistance: death and the cultural construction of agency in Himalayan mountaineering', *Representations,* no. 59, Summer, pp.135–62.

Weathers, Beck with Stephen G. Michaud 2000, *Left for Dead: My Journey Home from Everest,* Villard Books.

Newspaper articles

Kimmelman, Michael 1999, 'NOT because it's there', *The New York Times,* 6 June,
http://query.nytimes.com/gst/fullpage.html?sec=travel&res=9F03E2DC153EF935A35755C0A96F958260&n=Top%2fReference%2fTimes%20Topics%2fPeople%2fK%2fKimmelman%2c%20Michael

An article about changing attitudes to mountains; it mentions Into Thin Air.

Rothchild, John 2006, 'High jinks', *The New York Times,* 3 December, review of *No Shortcuts to the Top* by Ed Viesturs with David Roberts,
http://www.nytimes.com/2006/12/03/books/Rothchild.t.html?ei=5070&en=142e729db8c7dc6d&ex=1187841600&adxnnl=1&adxnnlx=1187691418-Nw3On+Su8cn3X0e44iuDFQ